D1346479

FORCES '86

FORCES '86

Marshall Cavendish

Published by
Marshall Cavendish House
58 Old Compton Street,
London W1V 5PA

Edited and designed by
DPM Services Ltd
19 Short's Gardens
London WC2H 9AT

Editor	Mark Dartford
Art Editor	Graham Beehag
Editorial Consultant	Geoffrey Cornish
Production Controller	Steve Roberts
Picture Research	John Moore/MARS

Printed and bound in Italy by
New Interlitho s.p.a.

CONTENTS

**RAF BAe Hawk trainer/air defence aircraft in Echelon
formation.**

INTRODUCTION

With the opening of the new airport at Mount Pleasant on the Falklands, and a greater degree of stability thus assured in the South Atlantic for the time being, Forces '86 looks to the future of Britain's military services and personnel in the broader context of world affairs, both at home and abroad.

A major NATO exercise in Europe has given planners and tacticians much food for thought over the coming months in regard to the strengths and weaknesses of Britain's armoured defence in Europe. Also, besides re-evaluating our air capability, Forces '86 looks at a unique and historic regiment, examines the futuristic concept of Star Wars from a British standpoint, and introduces a special illustrated feature on one of the Navy's most secret weapons – the submarine.

A special annual review section outlines in brief the year's main activities and events across the military spectrum, to give an up-to-date and balanced picture of Britain's Forces for 1986.

RAF Regiment CVR(T) Scorpion on manoeuvre.

Chapter 1

EXERCISE EUROPE: LIONHEART

1984 saw the biggest invasion of Europe carried out since the Second World War, involving nearly 120,000 British troops alone in an exercise designed to test and stretch the NATO response to a major Soviet bloc offensive in Europe.

Challenger Main Battle Tanks of 'A' Sqn, Royal Hussars during Exercise Lionheart. The yellow flag shows the tank has been 'knocked out' by umpires' decision.

The British army chose September to stage its massive Exercise Lionheart 84 not only because it is the traditional month for warfare in Europe – after the grain has been harvested and before the winter makes the battlefields unuseable – but also because the holidays would be over and the tourists would no longer be filling the roads of northern Europe and the cross channel ferries on which the army depends for getting its reinforcements to BAOR.

This combination of military needs in a civilian framework typified the exercise for it was essentially designed to see how quickly and efficiently Britain's civilian-soldiers, the Territorial Army, could get into action. And, since it was peacetime, the planners had to take into account factors which would not arise in wartime. The "terriers" all had to get a fortnight off from work at the same time, tickets had to be bought for each one travelling on the channel ferries, road convoys had to fit into normal traffic patterns and care had to be taken not to do too much damage to farmland – although £8 million of the exercise's total cost of £13 million was allocated to damage compensation.

Within these constraints they staged the largest British army field exercise since the end of World War I, involving 131,565 troops of whom 118,200 were British, 13,200 coming from other NATO forces with 165 specialist troops from the Commonwealth. Some indication of the logistical problems posed by movement and supply of all these men may be gathered from the fact that they needed among other things one and a half million sets of rations, two and a half million rounds of blank ammunition, 16 million litres of fuel, 120,000 thunderflashes, and 1,000 tons of plastic explosive.

LIONHEART succeeds CRUSADER

In order to cope with these problems, planning for Lionheart started shortly after the finish of its predecessor, Crusader, in 1980. In June 1984, Exercise Javelin was held purely to test the organisation which had been evolved to command, control and umpire the main exercise and this, in itself, entailed the building of a semi-permanent 12 acre camp to house the 2000 control staff and their equipment at Hildesheim in Germany.

It would be wrong to look on Lionheart as an isolated exercise. It was in fact part of a series of major exercises carried out by NATO, some of them overlapping, which were given the name "Autumn Forge 84". Lionheart itself consisted of two separate main exer-

Convoy of Scorpion-family vehicles joins civilian traffic on the road to the North German 'front'.

cises: "Full Flow" and "Spearpoint", and the concurrent testing of a whole range of new battle equipment

The scenario in which Lionheart was staged like some great theatrical production stipulated a period of acute political tension between the Warsaw Pact countries and NATO leading to an outbreak of conventional – not nuclear – warfare in Europe. The purpose therefore of "Full Flow", the first part of Lionheart, was threefold: to establish lines of communication for British reinforcements through Belgium, Holland and Germany, to get the reinforcements and their equipment across the channel and up to the front, and to conduct exercises in defending army and RAF installations in the "Rear Combat Zone and Communications Zone."

"Full Flow" was followed by "Spearpoint", a simulation of a major land and air battle over some 3,600 square miles of Lower Saxony, involving all the latest "kit" of modern warfare.

Operation FULL FLOW rolls into gear

"Full Flow" formally started on September 3rd, anniversary of the start of World War Two. The first troops to move were 270 men of the 2nd Battalion of the Royal Irish Rangers who, with 70 vehicles including half a dozen armoured cars started to set up the lines of communication along which 57,000 men were to move.

It took nearly a week to establish these lines of communication in Belgium, the Netherlands and the Rhine area. Then, from the 10th to the 15th of September, the main movement of Regular army reinforcements took place. They consisted mainly of the 2nd Infantry Division whose job is to protect the rear areas from saboteurs and infiltrators in time of war. Some 12,000 men and women of the RAF also went across to assist in the RAF's own exercise "Cold Fire" which was staged alongside and took part in Lionheart.

Then, on Friday September 14th, it was the turn of the Territorials and the Reservists. Men and women who had gone to work that morning as labourers, bank clerks, stockbrokers and farmers, reported for duty at their drill halls and depots that night as members of the armed forces on their way – theoretically – to war.

Units complete with their vehicles, PUE – prepacked unit equipment – and personal equipment which included face blacking supplied by Max Factor, moved down to the channel ports of Dover and Folkestone and other ports on the east coast where they boarded military transports and ferries and sailed for Ostend and Zeebrugge. More than 23,000 troops and 14,000 vehicles were transported by sea. The remainder, including the Reservists and reinforcements who were going to specific units were flown to civilian airports at Brussels and Dusseldorf and the RAF bases at Gutersloh and Wildenrath in Germany.

Soldier in full Nuclear, Biological, Chemical protection clothing, with Self Loading Rifle. British forces were virtually the only participants who spent most of the exercise in NBC suits, as they would in a real battle.

Above: Parachute Regiment equipment boarding a roll-on, roll-off ferry prior to crossing the channel as part of operation Full Flow, the deployment of British forces and material from the UK to support the Rhine Army. Left: After the machines, the men. Paras assemble to board coaches in London bound for the ports and airports. Because of the shortage of allocated road space, the easiest part of the operation was probably the crossings themselves. Above right: German Pioneers ferry British Paratroops across the Rhine following simulated Warsaw Pact destructon of the bridges.

Apart from the normal confusion attendant on any large scale military movement this part of the operation worked sweetly with the soldiers happily taking advantage of the civilian ferries' duty free shops. But on the other side things began to get complicated. it was planned that the troop convoys moving from the Belgian ports to their deployment positions in the North German Plain would move in the wartime formation of 150 vehicles to a convoy with 100 yards between vehicles on the autoroutes and half the distance on other roads. It was timed that the troop convoys would cover 30

miles in an hour while heavier, slower vehicles covered 24 miles.

20 minute window

The size and the speed of the convoys were dictated by the fact that because only a certain number of routes have been allocated to the British Army by Belgium and the Netherlands for use in wartime the British would have access to a given stretch of road for only about twenty minutes in one hour, the remaining time being allocated to the vehicles of other allies. Therefore the whole of a single British convoy has to be capable of passing a given spot within those twenty minutes.

The plans to do this may look splendid on paper but as any soldier knows, nothing as complicated as that ever works properly. And so it was with Lionheart. Soon there were jams and units which should have had priority fell seriously behind with their timetable. As one old sweat said, looking gloomily at the rain from the back of his lorry: "Its like the M1 with roadworks on a Bank Holiday." And, although most units had taken up their positions within 48 hours of leaving their drill halls

it took some as long as three days.

The first stop on the route was the staging area at Leuth near Venlo on the Dutch border where there was a mandatory six hour minimum halt for fuel, food and rest. Leuth, which five days of continuous rain had made cold, muddy and gloomy was nonetheless a welcome sight for the civilian warriors. There were big khakhi mess tents with hot food in generous ladlefulls but no matter how many prizes the chefs of the Army Catering Corps may win, food in the field soon returns to basics. There were latrines painted an extraordinary bright green, plastic petrol containers spreading across the ground like black blancmange, all the impediments of modern warfare.

Some of the reinforcements were flown directly to their battle stations by Chinook helicopters but most headed for the bridges crossing the Rhine only to discover that they had been "destroyed by sabotage" and the only way over the river was by the German Army's M2 ferries. From September 17th to the 19th these ferries, operating at five crossing points, ferried 15,000 troops and 8,000 vehicles – a considerable feat.

Sea crossings designed to simulate combat conditions

The crossings were conducted in conditions as close to actual combat as the planners could make them without using live ammunition and were part of the aim of General Sir Nigel Bagnall, Commander in Chief BAOR, to simulate the state of affairs that would apply during the first few days of a European war.

For some men the conditions were too realistic and when they arrived at their designated positions after two and sometimes three days travelling and were then asked to prepare defenses it became evident that they were not "combat-fit". The Reservists suffered more than the Territorials in this respect for they only do one day's training a year and that is taken up mainly with checking their equipment. Moreover, as many of them had left the Regular forces some years before they were not only unfit but had not been trained to use the equipment introduced in the last few years.

Furthermore the defensive positions the newly arrived troops were ordered to construct were not the old fashioned slit trenches quickly dug with entrenching tools. The lessons learnt in the Falklands of what can happen when a "sanger" is hit by an anti-tank rocket and the formidable power of new Soviet artillery have dictated a return to almost World War I style protective bunkers.

This has posed its own logistics problem, for the corrugated iron, stakes and sandbags needed to build these bunkers all need ferrying up to the front line and would prove an added burden for infantrymen already as they say, "cream-crackered". The opportunity was therefore taken to use Lionheart to test mechanical trench diggers and new types of light-weight but tough trench building material. The lessons of this exercise are still being digested but one cannot help thinking that such luxuries would be among the first things to disappear from the supply lines in a real war and the front line troops would resort to the time-honoured practise of tearing off the roofs of nearby barns to provide the material for their bunkers.

That of course is impossible in peacetime and great care was taken not to alienate the German public. General Bagnall issued an order to the troops saying: "You must all appreciate the tolerance and the goodwill of the German people, especially the landowners and farmers over whose land you are exercising. Instructions governing the use of land have been made clear and I ask you all to comply with them with respect and understanding."

Problems of making war in peace

Naturally enough, there were problems: road accidents involving heavy equipment and walls which came off second best after encounters with tanks slewing on narrow village streets. And no farmer likes to see his fields of winter crops churned into mud by Main Battle Tanks. But everybody knows that compensation is paid both swiftly and generously. The only real protests came

Above: RAEC Escort officer with a Chieftain of the Queen's Royal Irish Hussars having its steering disk renewed in the field during Lionheart. Constant mechanical repairs are an essential feature of armoured warfare: an unserviceable tank is not only useless, but can slow down an advance or halt a convoy.

from anti-war demonstrators who blocked some roads, cut telephone wires and sprayed vehicles with paint. They were dealt with by the German police.

There were many aspects to "Full Flow" involving not only the speedy transport of fighting men to the "sharp end" but the organisation of the infrastructure needed to keep an army in the field. For example Territorials of 68 Company of the Royal Pioneer Corps from Northampton built and operated a Prisoner of War cage to hold "enemy" forces captured during the exercise. Its first occupants were a group of "saboteurs" captured while trying to interrupt communications behind the lines. Territorial soldiers of the 4th Battalion of the Royal Irish Rangers from Portadown practised the reception, interrogation and guarding of the prisoners. It is interesting to note that Northern Ireland does have

Above: Trooper of 'B' Company, 1st Light Infantry Number Four Platoon with a General Purpose Machine Gun (GPMG) in a slit trench. Generally perceived as a mobile, armoured battlefield the North German plains afford little cover. In the event of a conventional war in Northern Europe, infantry position would have to be dug-in at each troop movement.

a Territorial force quite outside the context of the Ulster Defence Regiment and the security situation in the province.

"Full Flow" continued until 21st September and for its last four days ran concurrently with "Spearpoint" which started on the 17th with the westerly movement of a Panzer Division made up of German, American and Dutch tanks to oppose the build-up of British troops. "Spearpoint" involved more than 100,000 British and Allied troops. 480 Main Battle Tanks, 2,375 other tracked vehicles and 12,800 wheeled vehicles. The whole exercise was commanded by Lt. General Sir Martin Farndale from the Hildesheim headquarters and was based on the scenario that the Orange (Warsaw Pact Force) was attacking the Blue (NATO Force) with an armoured thrust supported by Special Forces.

In order to maintain control of the exercise the Orange forces were directed from Hildesheim but the Blue forces were allowed "free play" with its divisional commanders permitted to react to the Orange force's manoeuvres thus giving them every opportunity within the rules of the exercise to display their initiative and power of command. The Orange tanks rumbled across the exercise border in the early hours of the 18th September pushing back the Blue's reconnaissance patrols before coming up against the covering forces.

At the same time the Orange Special forces, built round the British 5th Airborne Brigade which included both the 10th Princess Mary's Own Gurkha Rifles and the SAS as well as several Territorial infantry battalions, acted as paratroop and helicopter-lifted raiding forces. They simulated the role of Russia's crack "Spetsnaz" troops, the Soviet equivalent of the SAS.

The Orange tanks pushed back Blue's covering forces drawn from tank units of both the 3rd and 4th Armoured Divisions. By dusk on the first day of the invasion these units had fallen back to the main defensive position. The battle for this position went on until 22nd

Milan anti-tank missile

Detachable protective cap · Launch tube · Warhead · Priming fuze · Motor · Decoder · I.R. day tracer · Piston · Gas generator · Detachable protective cap · Gyro · Wire spool · I.R. night tracer

September. The terrain helped the anti-tank forces of the defenders and the invading force made slow progress being harried not only by the Chieftain and new Challenger tanks of the defenders but also by the 6th Airmobile Brigade which was used with great imagination to plug the gaps forced open by the Orange tanks.

Armed with the Milan anti-tank weapon which was such a success in the Falklands the brigade's two infantry battalions were ferried around the battlefield by RAF Chinooks and Pumas. The cooperation between the brigade and the RAF was one of the great successes of the exercise and the brigade performed impressively.

"Russian" Special Forces harrass Blue's rear

While the tanks and artillery were slogging it out up front a different sort of war was being fought behind the lines with Orange's "Spetsnaz" troops mounting some ninety actions every twenty four hours against Blue's

lines of communications and installations – including nuclear weapons stocks. The importance of this aspect of modern warfare has been recognised and, where ten years ago troops at these installations would have been expected to protect themselves, now a whole infantry division has been allocated to guard against "Spetsnaz" operations, airmobile raids and "sleeping" saboteurs. This division, the 2nd Infantry Division, consists of one Regular and two Territorial brigades and is organised so that it not only provides standing guards but also has motorised quick reaction forces stationed at key points ready to attack enemy troops helicoptered or parachuted behind the lines. For Lionheart the division also had Home Defence Brigade placed under its command.

The first phase of the field exercise continued until 22nd September with that weekend being given over to the recouping of forces for the next stage of the battle – Blue forces counter-attack. It also gave the good citizens of the area a respite from the noise of the tanks and the mock artillery.

Blue force then unleashed its full power against the enemy. The main battle tanks, the 175mm guns and the RAF's Harriers and Tornados pounded the retreating Orange units. The Harriers moved out from their parent airfields to operate singly from camouflaged positions in woods and fields and, performing their aerial ballet act, spread thousands of anti-tank bomblets over the Orange armour.

While the Harriers and Army Air Corps Lynx helicopters armed with TOW anti tank weapons popped up all over the battlefield, the Tornados ranged further afield to attack the enemy's second and third echelons before they could reach the front line. At the same time Rapier anti-aircraft missiles – another success of the Falkland conflict – and German air defence cannon guarded the Blue Forces.

LIONHEART goes non-nuclear

What was unusual about Lionheart was that it did not end in a nuclear exchange. Lt. General Farndale had insisted on realism when he prepared the plot of his drama and, although NATO is still committed to the use of nuclear weapons in order to avoid defeat, current military thinking is tending to look towards non-nuclear armaments; more powerful guns, tanks and aircraft, to dissuade the Russians from going to war.

Lionheart was therefore used not only as a test of men and the means of getting them from civvy street in Britain to the battlefield of Northern Europe – over which their ancestors have fought so many times – but also of new tactics and new weapons.

Many lessons were learnt in the Falklands, especially the value of large helicopters for moving men and heavy loads over difficult terrain and the need for quickfiring guns to act as "goalkeepers" against low flying aircraft which have evaded the missile defences.

The helicopter lesson was well applied in Lionheart with Chinooks moving around the battlefield with large loads slung under their bellies. But strangely enough, while the Royal Navy responded quickly to the need for a cannon air-defence system and the German, Dutch and American units involved in Lionheart were well equipped such systems mounted on tracked vehicles as well as missile systems, the British Army has put all its eggs in the Rapier basket.

This is not meant to disparage the Rapier; it is a highly effective system and the new tracked Rapier manned by only three men and mounted on a single vehicle which was used in Lionheart is a far more effective sys-

Cont. p. 22

Cont. p. 22

Below: Tornado of RAF Germany deployed off the main runway during Exercise Coldfire, the air power exercise run in conjunction with Lionheart to test the ability of the RAF to back up an assault in Europe.

WHERE ARE THEY NOW?

2 Para

In March 1985 Private Simon Collyer of 2 Para was one of four men from his battalion who went to Denmark to take part in a physical training course run by the Danish Special Forces. Known as the Danish Patrol Course, the training took 2 months. As well as Danish soldiers, other course members included four US Home Guards. The British contingent were involved as part of a reciprocal arrangement. The Danish Special Forces carry out some of their training with the SAS in the Brecon Beacons and elsewhere.

The days of the course were crammed with activity, many beginning with an hour and a half of swimming tests after a 6.30 AM roll-call.

"There was an awful lot of swimming and swimming tests. In the first week we had to qualify to continue the course with a basic swimming test of 300 metres in eight minutes. We also had to qualify on what was called the Bronze Circuit, a series of seven exercises that you had to get round three times in under twelve minutes. It was very hard. We'd just come back from Ireland, and our fitness wasn't too good, but we all improved quite a lot towards the end. After that we had five minutes rest, then straight into a one and a half mile road run, in boots and denims. It was the equivalent of our BFT (battle fitness test).

As we progressed with the swimming we had to do things like survival swimming – that included doing fifteen hundred metres with clothes on. We did swimming Monday, Tuesday and Wednesday each week. On Tuesday and Thursday nights we did night navex (navigation exercises), finishing at about 9 the next morning, then working on until 12. We were in a place called Aalborg in the north, it's about 30 kilometres from the sea. The Danish Special Forces training with us were called the Jaeger Korps – meaning Hunter Corps. As a corps they do everything, including HALO (High Altitude Low Opening parachute drops), diving – a lot of water work. We did work with rubber boats and paddles. The first thing we learned was capsize drill, first on dry land, and then in the water. Later we were dropped by ship about one and a half kilometres from the shore on a night paddling exercise. We had to put men into the beach, blow up a railway, then get back out to be picked up by helicopters. They were very keen on demolitions, blowing things up. Also map reading, at which they're very good. They do a lot of orienteering both on and off duty. Some of the Danes seem to be able just to look at a map once, fold it up and put it in their pocket, and walk about 15 kilometres without looking at it again. The last exercise we did was over

Below: The Prince of Wales at a remembrance ceremony in Normandy with past and present members of the Parachute Regiment to mark the fortieth anniversary of the D-Day invasion. 60 men 'dropped in' as part of the occasion.
Right: Parachute training continues. Note reserve chute on chest.

ten days. It included a simulated attack on vehicles using real explosives, plastics, to blow up vehicle wreckage. We learned how to blow links on chains, logs, axles, – you name it, we blew it up."

The contingent from 2 Para was a lot fitter when the two months with the Jaeger Korps were over. Some of the training, such as running, they found not too much of a challenge. Used to running up and down mountains in the UK, the Paras literally took the flat Danish land-

scape in their stride. Other things, such as swimming and boat work they had to catch up on. The biggest surprise? To discover that the Danish troops are members of their own trade union, have individual rooms in barracks, and have to pay for their food.

Remembering D-Day 1944

The most important ceremonial occasion of 1984 for the Parachute Regiment was the 40th anniversary of the D-

Left: Paras arriving on the DZ along with their equipment during training in the UK. Success in the exercise requires positioning aircraft so that a maximum number of men can be dropped in a given area in a short time. In June, 3 Para made a full battalion drop in just 10 minutes.

Day landings, on which D Company of 3 Para took part, flying out from Lineham to Caen, where they drew parachutes. From Caen they flew in two Mk 1 Hercules to Ranville, which had been the DZ for the 5th Parachute Brigade on D-Day, 1944. Now, on June 5th, forty years on, D Company dropped on the same DZ in front of a large crowd of veterans of the original campaign, and also in front of the Prince of Wales, the Colonel in Chief of the regiment. 60 men made the drop, forming up afterwards on the DZ and then going on to the 6th Airborne Division cemetery at Ranville for a church service. The same day everyone continued on to Merville, which had been a battery position taken by 9 Para on D-Day. There was a display by the Red Devils, followed by a march past.

The 6th of June was the big day of the anniversary ceremony. The Queen arrived in the royal yacht at Caen, and ceremonies were carried out on several of the beaches where the landings had taken place. Everyone involved was in No 2 dress, with the medals and swords of a full formal parade. 3 Para provided ushers for the service on the beach at Arromanches, and went on the following day to Pegasus Bridge, which had been taken on D-Day by Major John Howard, then of the Ox/ Bucks Light Infantry. Major Howard gave a battlefield tour of Pegasus Bridge. His regiment had been a part of the 6th Airborne Division. This division, in 1944, had contained the 4th and 5th Parachute Brigades, which each in turn contained three Parachute Battalions.

The company flew back from Caen that night and dropped at Hankley Common, near Aldershot. A barbecue was waiting for them on the common, and wives and girlfriends had been bussed out to celebrate with them.

Battalion in 10-minute drop

Later in June 3 Para carried out a full leading Parabattalion drop. Eight personnel aircraft were involved, plus seven heavy-drop aircraft and two stores aircraft. All aircraft were Hercules. The drop was part of an exercise that continued for a further three days. Almost 600 men jumped, and the aircraft used a close-formation technique that had not been used for a decade. By using triangular, mixed-altitude formations, it was possible to get the entire battalion on the ground in ten minutes instead of in the 45 minutes it would have taken with the single-stream technique usually employed over the last ten years. The close-formation approach, known as Limited Parachute Assault Capability (L-PAC) had lapsed as a technique in the mid 1970s, but has now been resurrected in line with a new government awareness of the potential need for a fast response force in hostage and siege situations. The aircraft come onto the DZ in 'Vics' or V-formations of three aircraft, with a minute between each formation. The aircraft will eventually be equipped with station-keeping equipment (SKE) allowing them to maintain their stations in the formation whatever the outside conditions are. In fact SKE, which is radar-based, will enable the aircraft to fly in virtually whatever numbers and types of formation they want. When SKE is in general use, the parachute assault capability will be full. Until then, it is known as a limited capability. As in the Trumpet Dance exercise in the USA in which 2 Para participated last year, the aim is for the green light to come on in every aircraft in the formation simultaneously.

Pathfinder Platoon

The routines, exercises, tours and ceremonies continue, but techniques and equipment are constantly updated. Now a new structure has been added to the Parachute Regiment in the form of the Pathfinder Platoon. Lieutenant Chris Waddington is a member of the new Platoon, which he joined from 2 Para. Pathfinder Platoon is based on the old patrol elements in both Battalions, whose job was to mark the DZ for the main force. The Platoon specializes in High Altitude Low Opening (HALO) drops, flying in and leaving the aircraft at 25,000 feet, and dropping in free-fall to around 3000 feet before opening the parachutes. High altitude aircraft noise is less likely to alert an enemy to an assault threat, though even at 3000 feet the crack of an opening 'chute can sound like a pistol shot. The members of the Pathfinder Platoon are equipped with a ten-minute oxygen bottle and two altimeters for HALO operations.

Without the oxygen equipment the body suffers from hypoxia – lack of oxygen – above about 12,000 feet, and after three minutes or so the brain begins to die. Pathfinder Platoon drops in ahead of the Brigade and sets out ground markers to guide the pilots and navigators. They place the marker panels and establish communications with the aircraft. The majority of the Pathfinders are from the Parachute Regiment, but there is also a small link unit from the Royal Signals. The Platoon has been formed because the skills needed for proficiency in HALO drops need to be practised all the time. A six month tour in Northern Ireland or Belize would be too disruptive. Once the drop has been made, the Pathfinder Platoon becomes an independent recconnoitring unit for the Brigadier in charge of the newly formed 5th Airborne Brigade. The Platoon is independent of the three Battalions. As soon as the Brigade is on the ground, the Pathfinders push forward, setting up observation posts, carrying out medium range recconnaissance, and possibly carrying out raids, with the use of demolition materials. The 27 members of the Pathfinder Platoon are already undergoing special training for these tasks.

tem than the towed version used in the Falklands. The towed version takes an hour to get into action and this delay contributed to the disaster at Bluff Cove when the Argentines bombed *Sir Galahad* and *Sir Tristram*. The tracked version is much faster but it is not as fast into action as the German and Dutch Gepard and the American Vulcan self-propelled air-defence systems. Observers believe that one of the main lessons learnt from Lionheart was the need for such a system in the British army to work with the Rapiers.

Of the new tanks taking part in the exercise, the British Challenger, fast and agile, was most impressive – but only one of the eight armoured regiments were equipped with it. The remainder still have the now ageing Chieftains. The Americans who had flown in their 1st "Tiger" Brigade of the 2nd (US) Armoured Division "Hell on Wheels" from Texas to Luxembourg as part of their "Reforger 84" exercise, had picked up their Abrams from their tankparks in Europe. This tank also performed well and, equipped with a laser firing simulator on its main gun, eased the umpire's task when claiming hits.

British armoured innovations tried in the field

Another British armoured vehicle still in the process of being accepted by the army is the MCV-80. It was having what amounted to a run-out to see how it will be used in battle. A cross between a light tank and an armoured personnel carrier, it is armed with a 30mm Rarden cannon and can carry eight infantrymen. Unlike the comparable American M2 Bradley and the West German Marder which also took part in Lionheart and the Soviet equivalent, the MCV-80 does not have firing ports for the infantry and neither is it fitted with anti tank missiles. It will be interesting to see how this vehicle is developed and how it is used.

Among the non-tracked vehicles the new British wheeled armoured personnel carrier, the AT-105 Saxon, was given its first test in a European exercise. The Saxons have a crew of two and carry eight infantrymen and, although they are ugly looking brutes, they proved themselves during Lionheart and were well-liked by the soldiers. This is just as well for the army needs 1,000 of them and they will be issued to Territorial as well as Regular battalions.

The army's procurement department also took the opportunity to try out the personal equipment being developed for the introduction of the new 5.56mm family of small arms and which will considerably change the appearance of the British soldier at war. There were none of the new weapons available but some troops were equipped with the experimental webbing developed to complement the new guns. The new plastic helmet designed to give protection both by its modern materials and redesigned shape, was also on trial. These trials under "battle" conditions are important for what might seem an excellent piece of kit in the barracks often proves to be useless in the field.

Evaluating LIONHEART

The lessons of Lionheart will take some time to evaluate. But some are already evident – in fact became evident before the exercise was a couple of days old. The first and probably the most important is the need to get the reinforcing troops to their battle positions fresh enough to fight. General Bagnall said that "Full Flow" had gone remarkably well "but admitted that there had been some "hiccups". If there were some hiccups in peacetime then there will certainly be more in wartime with the Channel mined and the ports and roads under aerial attack. A complicated system of convoying would almost certainly break down under war conditions.

Tracked Rapier Missile System

What must be done therefore in order to get the troops forward quickly is to convince the Dutch and Belgians and Germans to open up more roads than they have so far allocated to the British force.

It was also immediately apparent that something would have to be done about the standard of training and fitness of the Reservists. A programme called Project Star has been put together over the last 18 months. It will give the Reservists at least a week's training every year. But it will remain voluntary and much serious thought has to be applied to this problem.

Another major problem is the festering state of relations between the media and the Ministry of Defence.

Above: Tracked Rapier, a system used principally by units of the Rhine Army, and designed to provide close range air defence for troops and armour on the move. Unlike the static version used in the Falklands, tracked Rapier can be deployed rapidly. Inset: Test firing sequence.

There has always been antagonism between the men who want to tell all about a war and those who want to reveal nothing. It was Lord Kitchener who once threatened to horsewhip war correspondents and in some quarters of the Ministry of Defence this attitude still persists. The quarrel broke out with fresh bitterness during the Falkland conflict and the system of guarded trust which had been built up between military

Top: A Saxon wheeled armoured personnel carrier of Arnhem Company, King's Own Borderers near Gehrenrode towards the end of the exercise. Lionheart was the first major outing for the vehicle. Above: Another recent addition to the British armoured arsenal. Royal Hussar Challenger MBTs (Main Battle Tanks), also on a major exercise for the first time in Lionheart.

correspondents and Whitehall collapsed in a welter of mutual recrimination with the MOD, frightened by the effect of the TV cameras on the Vietnam war, accusing the correspondents of trying to evade censorship and thereby endangering the British forces, and the media accusing the MOD of imposing censorship and restric-

Above: Cutaway of Scimitar Combat Reconnaissance Vehicle. Scimitar is armed with the highly-successful 30mm Rarden cannon, and can carry up to 165 rounds of ammunition on board, with a crew of three.

tions which were not only ridiculous and political but also harmful to the British cause.

There has been much fence-mending since then and a new system has been developed under which war correspondents are given access to restricted information in exchange for responsible self-censorship. The army set out to give the reporters covering Lionheart a good time and most of them were moderately well satisfied by the new system. However, the suspicion remains that if ever the shooting starts again with live ammunition relations between the media and the MOD will collapse once more. Military secrecy is simply not compatible with television.

The beauty of a large and complicated exercise such as Lionheart is that all these problems and their possible solutions can be tested under realistic conditions and despite General Bagnall's "hiccups" and the gloomy assessment by General Leopold Chalupa, the West German who is C-in-C Allied Forces Central Europe, that "we have made some small progress but there is still a large field of activities to improve", Lionheart was an undoubted success.

The planning of both sections of the exercise and its integration with other exercises taking place all over Europe displayed staff work of the highest quality.

Major logistical achievement

To get all those men from their home across the Channel, feed and equip them and send them up to their posi-

tions and then get them back again was a major logistical achievement. Moreover, apart from the usual soldiers' grumbles most of those involved tackled their jobs enthusiastically, none more so than the Blue force units who were given freedom to use their initiative under the imaginative scenario devised by Lt. Gen. Farndale.

One other plus that came out of the exercise was the cooperation between the various NATO forces involved with the German Dutch and American tank units working together and with Belgian, Dutch and German units cooperating with the British 2nd Infantry Division to secure the rear areas against attack and smoothing the passage of the British reinforcement by taking over traffic control duty, engineering work and a number of other infrastructure roles.

Back to work...

On Thursday, September 27th it was all over. The regular troops returned to their barracks to absorb the lessons they had learnt and the Terriers and Reservists made their way back to disperse at their Drill Halls. Then, on Monday morning, it was back to work. And someone, somewhere in the army, is already beginning to plan the next exercise due to be staged in 1989.

WHERE ARE THEY NOW?

3 Para

"You just get split up into your company groups. Off you go for six months. Time stands still for you. The world goes on, and you're out there." Lance Corporal Terry Kipling, and Private Michael Thomson, both of 3 Para, are talking about Belize. They accept the recurring tour philosophically, as they do their Northern Irish tours. It's the job they're trained for. So was the Falklands operation. But that is fading fast now. The soldier's life goes on, and it is not as glamorous as some of the newspapers and magazines and TV films make out. Everything is cyclical. New intakes come from basic training, go through the time honoured exercises and courses and begin their tours of duty. Men move up in rank. New ones have to be trained for their jobs. Fitness and operational training are unceasing, though a spell in Northern Ireland or Belize disrupts the regular parachute drops. When they get back to the UK they have to catch up on their drops and other skills not used in the streets of Belfast or the jungles of Belize.

Yet even out in Belize there are battle-group exercises of the sort that take up a large part of the UK routines. "You do exercises out there the same as in UK" says Sergeant Colin Dyer. "They last up to two weeks. We travel out in four tonners or Puma helicopters, it depends on the weather. You might go out as a company group, a section, or a whole battalion, depending on the scenario. They run three exercises out there in the six-month period. First of all they try out battle-group North, based on Airport Camp and Holdfast Camp, and battle-group South, based on Salamanca Camp and Rideau Camp in the south of the country, in the foothills. Finally they finish up with a Belize Garrison exercise in which everyone takes part, including the RAF, the REs (Royal Engineers), the artillery – everyone. You'll have an armoured unit in Scorpions and Scimitars. They'll be involved in fire support. The airforce will play the enemy and friendly forces, using the Harriers. The Navy plays a part in it. You don't actually see them, but there's always a guard ship on the coast. Of course, while all this is going on you still have to man the normal posts."

Special Kit for jungle patrols

Patrols and outpost manning continues throughout the six months. The RAF runs support with Puma and Chinook helicopters. The smaller Lynx, Gazelle and Scout helicopters are run by the Army Aviation Corps. Patrols and outposts are in touch by radio with the two main north and south signals offices, though where distances are too long for direct communication, special re-broadcasting units can go out into the forests and hills, effectively doubling the range of patrol signals. The

Above: Back to work – paratroops on a training exercise over Salisbury Plain.

rainy season starts in about May, and the humidity shoots up to energy-sapping levels. Jungle kit includes American boots with self-draining eyelets and a steel-protected sole (developed in Vietnam to deflect sharpened stakes). Recent refinements include inflatable tubes which can be placed in a cover to form an air-bed, and the latest style of bergen has a flexible metal back plate that can be easily moulded to the shape of the individual back. 'Millbank' water-purifying bags help keep the myriad tropical diseases at bay. After return to the UK each man has to carry cards stating he has been exposed to malaria and a disease carried by sandflies. This last card reads, "The bearer of this card has been in Be-

to carry out camp duties such as fatigues and guards; one to man OPs and patrols; one to carry on the never ending training, keeping up weapons skills. This is the unglamorous side of service life the public forgets about. The peak of excitement is a gentle foray to discourage Guatamalan farmers from clearing and planting on Belize territory. Everything is done by diplomacy. Men from both sides of the border meet at Treetops. The problem is sorted out. No-one back home even hears about it. On the Belize side, patrols go out sometimes for 24 hours, sometimes 8 days. They get wet, hot, bitten by insects. They might go into a village to conduct a census, tagged by children demanding biscuits. They speak to a headman through a Belize Defence Force interpreter. They patrol the long, straight, north to south border, weighed down with tropical kit and rations. At night they sleep under rough tents made from ponchos and branches, covered by mosquito nets. Wherever they touch the tent, the night rains pour in. They learn not to move in their sleep. They tick off the slowly passing days of the tour. "Time stands still for you. The world goes on, and you're out there."

Back in the UK the year has been characterized by "alert phases" as the anniversaries of IRA bombings come and go. Extra duties have included guarding exercises for strategic targets such as power stations, and there have been additional roles as guards and escorts for Cruise missiles.

Back in UK – guarding Cruise

And all over the country, from Salisbury Plain to the Isle of Man, the big bellied Hercules have dropped strings of paratroopers in company and battalion exercises. Some exercises have been small scale night drops, followed by close target recconnoitering. Others have been full-scale eight-day operations at full strength, covering all phases of war. Battalion exercises can involve upwards of 870 men, with 600 of them taking part in the actual drop. The main dropping zone for an operation of this scale measures 4000 metres by 1000 metres. A separate DZ is used for vehicles and other plant, about 1,500 metres away from the main DZ. All men in the regiment carry out four or five drops a year in training, in addition to up to four battalion drops. Because of the comprehensive support systems of a large scale operation, the rifleman carries less equipment than he does when taking part in a purely parachuting exercise. On a short drop operation each man carries everything needed for two days, including food and water as well as a share of the group's equipment. All this adds up to about 110 pounds, plus a support weapon, bringing the total to a staggering 125 lbs.

Some exercises recently have included a scenario in which hostages have to be rescued from a defended position, a response to real-life snatch operations carried out in recent years in various parts of the world.

lize within the last two years. Should any skin nodules or ulcers develop they may be cutaneous leishmaniasis." Occurrences of this disease are rare, but incurable. The flesh rots away after an incubation period of up to two years, resulting sometimes in gross disfigurement. Two men from 3 Para contracted the disease on the last Belize tour.

Sergeant Dyer was based at Salamanca Camp. The static observation post there rejoices in the name 'Treetops', and looks out over the border into Guatamala. There is not much to see: a village where a road tails off; a ditch. Guatamalan observers watch in the opposite direction.

Discouraging ambitious Guatamalan farmers

In the humid heat of the south the platoons rotate. One

Chapter 2
FORCES LIFE: JOINING UP

A blow-by-blow account of the gruelling process by which a raw young man is turned into a Royal Marine – from the day he first sets eyes on the tortuous course at Lympstone to his final passing out parade . . . if he makes it.

Royal Marine recruits on the assault course at the Commando Training Centre at Lympstone.

ympstone is beautifully sited on the Exe estuary. The camp sweeps down from the Exmouth road towards the water. But the new arrivals are all looking in the other direction when they get off the train. First the nets and walls of the assault course, then a steep rise. At the top, figures in denims doing machine gun drills. Beyond them, the brick accommodation blocks. The wind blows and it looks bleak. Some are already beginning to wish they had stayed at home.

There are two Potential Recruits Courses a week at Lympstone. They last two and a half days, and there are usually about 25 aspiring marines on each. Nearly all of them just walked into a recruiting office one day. Surprisingly the majority had jobs already. Their reasons for that momentous move break down into three main groups. There are those who already have family or friends in the Marine Corps. Inside information. They have been told by their uncles and brothers and mates that it's a great life – once you've finished basic training. The trouble is, the Marines' basic training is the longest of any service in the country, thirty weeks, almost eight punishing months. The second group want to join up because they fancy the active life, the sport and the action, the fabled fitness. The third group, larger than either of the others, are in love with the image, the idea of an ultimate elite. "They're just the best. That's all there is to it." "It's the price. The Green Beret." "I've just always wanted to be in the Marines." In civvy street they were in the building industry, butchers, platers, fitters, engineers, still at school.

At the recruiting office they all had a two hour test to make sure they could survive the 2½ days Potential Recruits Course to come. They had to prove they could read and write, and do three pull-ups on a bar. They were shown a film about training and going to a unit. Not designed to put anyone off. A month or so later they were on their way to Lympstone, looking at the assault course from the train.

After 2½ days some of them look distinctly frayed around the edges, but their enthusiasm was vociferous. It was hard, much harder than they had thought. They were shouted at. They had to get up at 5 am and clean the floor, clean the heads, make their beds, wash, and then clean the floor again. The corporal was convinced it had not been touched. But they were still keen, they had all got on well together, sleeping in the same big room, and they had done gym tests and an assault course.

Drop-out rate reduced

Later an officer explained how the most valuable function of the PRC was to give a chance to those who discover Marine life was definitely not for them to dip their toes in the water and retire gracefully. Before the PRC was instituted, the early opt-out rate was very much higher than at present, an expensive, time wasting business. The potential recruits were treated fairly gently in their 2½ days. Not so gently as to give them a totally false impression, but not so harshly as to scare them away at

the first hurdle either, unless they definitely wanted to give the Marines a miss. Physical potential was tested during the course by the PT staff under WO2 Scott.

"They can fail at that level. The whole idea of the PRC is to give them an idea of what to expect when they arrive, but also to give us an idea, so if they're not up to a certain standard we can look at them and say, 'He will never ever make a marine.' It's not just a matter of physical abilities. It's also a matter of his mental attitudes, his application. It doesn't matter how unfit they are really. If you see a person had determination, and is willing to try, and put some effort into it, then fair enough. The phsyical tests at this stage consist of pull-ups, press-ups, running ability, sit-ups – a series of tests, and also a series of obstacles we set up in the gym. It's a sort of mini-assault course."

At the end of the PRC the applicants are divided into three groups. The first consists of those who have a reasonable chance of coping with basic training. The second is those who are probably a little immature, could well fail the 30 week course at some point, but might be worth a second try in six months time. The third group are those the assessors consider faily certain to fail.

Above: Recruits at the end of a nine-mile speed march pull in to the base. Physical fitness is vital at Lympstone.

New boys' first day

Each new intake for basic training consists of a 'troop' of between 20 and 40 men. On the first day they officially join the camp, are sworn into the service, issued bedding and shown what to do with it, lectured on the security of personal belongings, and given the one and only free haircut of their service careers. In this induction phase they all live together in one area, numbers allowing, where they can be kept under the eye of their guardian corporal. Everything is happening at once. Lectures on everything from pay to personal hygiene, kit issues, drill on the square, rifle-butt fitting, medicals. They are taught the basics of self-sufficiency.

"You have to instruct them in the basics of life. Washing. Ironing. All the things that a lot of people regard as mum's work. They stay together in a large billet for two weeks, wearing orange shoulder flashes that serve the same purpose as L-plates, so that people know they're new and don't jump on them too hard."

At the end of the third week the troop moves from the induction block to a permanent block where they are billeted between six and eight to a room. They may well stay there for the remainder of their thirty weeks. Now the training proper begins. Looking back on this time, those about to finish the course remember it as a time of perpetual panic, exhaustion, homesickness, never having kit ready in time, going to bed way after midnight, trying to keep up with the cleaning and preparing. They are now members of Portsmouth Company, where they will remain until Week 15. The second half of the course will be spent as members of Chatham Company.

The fieldcraft exercises start in Week 1 with exercise First Step, a five-day introduction to living in the field, including a night exercise. Exercise Twosome, in Week 4 extends the fieldcraft to concealment, observation, night-movement, and the use of compass and maps at night as well as day. Both these first exercises take place on Woodbury Common. Weapon training has begun with the SLR rifle.

In Week 8 exercise Hunter's Moon includes advanced map-reading and stalking. Weapons training with blanks begins. They load-carry back 8 miles to camp, with 60 lb loads, including weapons.

Fieldcraft and tactical survival

In Week 11 they take part in survival and map-reading exercises on much more rugged terrain. There are three sites for this 4-day exercise, one on Exmoor (Omega Man), and two on Dartmoor, (Avon Stroll and Dart Venture). To prepare for this survival exercise each man has made up his own survival tin, going into Exmouth to buy items such as waterproof matches, rabbit snares, fishing tackle. Only a minimum of kit is carried, and no food is allowed. They are thoroughly searched before going into the field, and all snacks and chocolate confiscated. One of the reasons for this exercise is to give the recruits experience of going without food, so none is issued for the duration of the four days, unless the exercise takes place in winter, when some food is provided. A long insertion march of over 24 km is intended to give a sense of isolation to the sections, usually of four men plus a corporal. The march also burns up the calories, giving edge to the hunger. After the insertion march into rough countryside, each section (none of which are in contact with any others) constructs a survival area, gathers firewood, puts out traps and snares if possible, and holds fast for 12 hours. They then go into a series of day and night compass marches, probably covering as much as 60 km altogether. By the afternoon of the last full day they are all very tired and very hungry. Each pair of men is issued with a live rabbit. They are almost always hungry and desperate enough to kill the rabbit and eat everything including the nourishing organs which a few days previously they would have had great difficulty in stomaching.

Field exercises a welcome change from spit and polish

Despite the hardships, most of the recruits have looked

forward to the survival exercise in Week 11. Freedom from the constant struggle with 'personal admin' (cleaning and preparing kit) is welcome. For four days their kit consists of a boiler suit, boots, a shirt, a water bottle, a bin liner, the survival kit – usually a tobacco tin – and a woolly hat. No washing, shaving, or even taking clothes off. It is on this exercise that the NCOs and officers start to look for potential section leaders for the second half of the course. These are the men who may eventually show the leadership and initiative qualities to become 'diamonds' – wearing a red diamond to denote status – and may be in line for the covetted Queen's Badge award for the best recruit of the intake.

In Week 13 the troop does a week's work with the General Purpose Machine Gun (GPMG) at the Tregantle ranges at Tor Point across the river from Plymouth, with some earning marksman badges, which are to be re-won annually. Week 13 ends with the Baptist Run. The purpose of this is to test the men individually in all the important areas covered so far, to ascertain if they are ready to transfer to Chatham Company at the end of Week 15. All aspects of fieldcraft are tested, including field signals, first aid, and general admin – the maintenance and cleaning of all equipment in the field. Each day begins with an hour's PT followed by an inspection, with clean weapon and gear. This is one of the recruit's biggest problems, even at this stage of the course. The weekend ends with a speed march back to Lympstone.

Above left: Elementary mountaineering. Below left: Practice with the GPMG. Above: Workouts in the gymnasium are an essential part of the fitness course.

At this point a major shake out takes place to see who will carry on to the second half of the course. Some are back-trooped for another shot, though not necessarily all the way to Week 1. Some, who have already completed two Baptist Runs may get another try, and may not. Those suitable for continuing celebrate the end of their time in Portsmouth Company with a four-day 'resource and initiative' training session at Penhale in Cornwall. This includes climbing, abseiling, canoeing and orienteering, and is their first introduction to the all-important ropework taught by the Mountain Leaders.

Indoor gymnasium of cricket pitch size

Throughout the first half of the course the troop has spent a considerable amount of time with the PT Wing. The PT course that they follow is as carefully thought out as any military tactic, and is backed up by what must be one of the finest gymnasium complexes in Europe. The main gymnasium is large enough to house a cricket match, and is divisible into a number of flexible areas by means of drop nets. A secondary gym houses weight-lifting equipment and machinery, and is flanked by a superb climbing wall. Elsewhere in the complex is a 33 m swimming pool and a series of squash courts.

WO2 Scott is the Sergeant Major of PT Wing. "We start with a programme known as Initial Military Fitness (IMF), which is the old gymnasium type of PTE which used to be done in schools, quite a few years ago, called the Swedish System."

In the big gymnasium a block of about thirty recruits are concentrating very hard. All are dressed in white – white collarless gym shirt, white shorts, white gym shoes. A small team of very muscular gym instructors calls out the orders, and the ranks of recruits swing arms, step back, to the side, forward, arms up – a constant flow of movements. It is an old-fashioned routine, but the concentration is total.

"It's a regimented type of PT where they form up in teams, and all do the exercises at the same time. We're trying to foster basic fitness, coordination, alertness of the mind, team spirit. Plus discipline and posture. But the top basic skills are rope climbing, and how to apply themselves physically to any basic task. Coupled with that we'd be doing vaulting and that kind of thing, and we'd also be running and swimming."

All the runs are done in boots and denims. From the very beginning a pace of 8 minutes to the mile is set. This pace does not change throughout the 30 weeks of training. What does change is the terrain and the distance.

"We start off at about a mile and a half, building up in the first ten weeks to three to four miles. They run in a group, which is very different from running as an individual. From day one we try to run at the pace of 8

Left: Spectacular, if inaccurate, method of firing a GPMG. In a real war, the line between acts of courage and carelessness can be very narrow indeed. Above: Putting in some practice against armour with, left, a Carl Gustav anti-tank weapon and right, the GPMG.

minutes per mile. Not everyone can manage it at first, and we can drop back a notch.

Throughout their whole training the recruits have about twenty-two periods of swimming. Some have to start from scratch, and we teach them to swim. Each period is forty minutes. The first period is at 8 o'clock in the morning. We finish at 16.30. Of course their PT is coupled with their normal military training. They cannot be drafted to an operational unit until they reach a certain swimming standard. The standard test – BST, Battle Swimming Test – is that in full fighting order they must jump off an eight foot board into the deep end, swim two lengths, jettison their equipment without touching the side at the end of that two lengths, and remain afloat for three minutes. The whole lot takes three minutes. The practical side of that is, if they had to leap from a landing craft, and take out a beach . . . if they can't do that they can't be drafted. Our main criterion is to get them to swim in those conditions. If we can do that, then we're happy."

A break . . . at last

The last day of Week 15 is devoted to a Parents' Day, followed by a long weekend leave. Many recruits find the leave a great problem. They are back home for the first time, unless a major public holiday such as Christmas has intervened. A home break seems to excavate all the old home-sickness. When Christmas does fall before the halfway point of the course, more recruits than usual decide to opt out. For ordinary recruits this is not easy, and requires a money payment. Junior recruits, who follow the same course but begin it at 16 years old can opt out at any time. In all, the failure and opt-out rate seems to hover around 40 percent of the original intake.

Infantry Phase

Part Two of the course is known as the Infantry Phase. Weapons training is expanded to include anti-tank weapons, mortars and grenades. Exercises and practices now include live rounds with increasing frequency. In Week 18 anti-tank training and ambushing are learned and practiced. All-night exercises, sleeping out in bivouacs, can be followed by days of lessons. After the brief break exhaustion sets in again. Questioned about this period, those about to finish the course remember best the constant harassment. However fit they become, the tasks become harder, the speed marches longer. They complain that they had not realized how hard the course would become mentally as well as physically. Several say they are glad to have almost completed the course, but could not, with the benefit of hindsight, bear the idea of going through it all again. The aggro – being shouted at from pillar to post – never stops. You work flat out, and they still shout at you.

The physical training now gets intense. At the PT Wing, when 32 periods of Swedish training had been completed in the first half of the course, it was followed

Cont. p. 38

WHERE ARE THEY NOW?
Mike Smith, 40 Commando, RN.

There is a world of difference between Cyprus and Brunei. 40 Commando of the Royal Marine Corps have operated in both countries since mid-1984. The Cyprus tour was a six-month stint with the United Nations peace keeping force, undertaken by the entire Commando, between 600 and 700 men. Only a hundred or so men went to Brunei, for a six-week training exercise in tropical jungle conditions. Corporal Mike Smith and Marine Andrew Seal were on both trips.

Mike Smith has been in the Marines for 8 years, with a further 4½ years as a civilian Marine reserve before joining up. He took part in the Falklands campaign, manning observation posts for the Commando forward of San Carlos. He was at the OPs for the duration of the campaign, eventually being pulled back to Fox Bay before embarking once more for the UK. Like many men who were in the Falklands, he is a little impatient of questions about it now, three years later. It was his job to do what he did. He went there, did the job, came back. Life in the Commando goes on. The Falklands campaign is a thing of the past. He claims not to remember much about it.

It is not common for the Marines to carry out a Cyprus tour. 41 Commando had been there five years previously. 40 Commando went out in June 1984. Their task was to patrol the British sector of the UN Buffer Zone, and also to help protect the British Sovereign Base at Dhekelia. The diplomatic niceties of the UN peace-keeping, essential though they are in the delicate Cyprus situation, do not make for exciting soldiering. The British sector runs from Nicosia to the Troodos mountains, a 35 km stretch of the 217 km 'Green Line'. 40 Commando were based on three camps spread out across the sector. They traded their green Marine Corps berets for the light blue berets of the UN force, and added UN shoulder flashes to their shirts. In the dry heat of Cyprus, with summer temperatures soaring well above 100F, the Commando carried out the set routines of patrolling and manning observation posts.

"You maintain a surveillance over no-man's land, basically. In some parts it's only 50 metres at most between the Greeks and the Turks. In other parts it's miles. You have to maintain the status quo. You're in the Buffer Zone – that's UN property. You patrol on foot or by Landrover, maybe eight men at a time.

Right: Jungle training is still an important part of British military training, despite the primary role in Northern Europe. Belize and Brunei are tough assignments.

You're showing a presence – as opposed to doing anything."

UN mission unadventurous

Without exactly saying so, Corporal Smith gives the impression that the lack of action became a little tedious. Each patrol was based on a task, such as meeting a farmer, or overseeing crop harvesting. Sometimes the patrols had support from army helicopters or armoured vehicles such as Ferret Scout cars, from other British units. There were no joint patrols with UN troops from other countries, whom they only saw when operating at the far ends of the British sector. The sector is manned 24 hours a day, seven days a week. In the first weeks the work-load was heavy, with a rigorous watch system and no time off for recreation. Gradually, as routines became established, they could have occasional time off. One of the tasks was to escort visitors to the British Military Cemetery, where there are graves of British servicemen from the Second World War, from the time of the EOKA troubles, and from the time of the 1974 Turkish invasion. The cemetery lies between Nicosia and its now derelict airport, and is flanked by manned Turkish and Greek military positions. Another task was

to escort and oversee Greeks and some Turks who came in by special arrangement to maintain the gardens of houses which were in no-man's land, and no longer inhabited.

Marine commandos are highly trained troops, kept at a peak level of physical fitness and military preparedness. For some the Cyprus posting was boring, a waste of a Commando unit. Despite the heat, which reached 120F at one point, a lot of surplus energy was channelled into sports and competitions. 40 Commando became Island champions at rugby, swimming, volley-ball and six-a-side hockey. They also excelled in soccer and cross-country running, and came second in the gruelling Cyprus Walkabout, a two-day event in which teams have to run from sea level to the peak of Mount Olympus at 6,000 feet, and back again, over rough mountain tracks. The total distance is around 60 miles and temperatures were in the 90s.

Andrew Seal, 40 Commando, RN.

Marine Andrew Seal won the 3,000 metres steeplechase as part of the team that won the Army (Cyprus) Inter Unit Athletics Championships.

As an athlete in demand for inter-unit competitions,

Above: Royal Marines doing duty as part of the United Nations peace keeping force in Cyprus. Note berets and badges.

Andrew Seal reckons himself lucky to have spent only about two months of the six months tour carrying out patrol duties. The rest of the time he was competing or training. He was also in one of the 40 Commando teams which took first and second places in the twice-yearly UN Military Skills Competition. In two days of tests competitors demonstrate various facets of field-craft, carry out an OP, and continue with physical tests that begin with an assault course, go on to a 9 mile speed march, and end with a shooting contest.

The Cyprus tour ended in mid-December, 1984. The patrols and OPs seemed repetitive and low-key, but the constant presence of the Greek and Turkish units facing one another across the Buffer Zone was a daily reminder of the necessity for a third force between the lines. Once, in October, a freak storm flooded roads and washed live mines down from the hillsides, underlining the fact that the confrontation was no exercise, and that Cyprus had been the scene of much violence in the past, and could be so again. The six months up, 40 Commando returned to their permanent base at Taunton with something like a sigh of relief.

"I wouldn't rush back there, I'll tell you that. I think it's about number fifty in my list of priorities. I think it holds you back in your training too. You'd have benefited more spending six months here in the UK. As a result, since coming back the unit's been rushed off its feet retraining for their normal role."

Left: Royal Marine Andrew Seal putting a brave face on the surroundings in Brunei.

by eight periods of military skills, four inside and four outside. They were in the form of mini-assault courses, beams and boxes at various heights, and tunnels. There followed a further 18 periods of Battle Fitness Training in the bottom field. The obstacles were far larger then they had ever come across before. However the skills they've learned on the smaller obstacles relate to the larger ones. They just have to dredge up extra effort. As well as the assault course there are other types of exercise. Split into groups, one group would do the assault course, another would be performing circuits, the third would climb the thirty-foot ropes. There is an emphasis on rope-climbing. The practical application rests in the fact that the Marines' main form of transport is the helicopter. If the helicopter cannot land to pick you up because of the terrain, the marines have to climb up a rope to get aboard. If one person cannot get up the rope in full equipment, then he is going to hold everyone else up.

Pick up a man, and his equipment and . . . run

"On Week 22 the recruits finish their Battle Fitness Training. During all this time they have been doing speed-marches and runs as well as the other training. By Week 22 we hope they can do six-mile runs. They now have a series of tests to make sure they've reached the required standard on the assault course, the 30 foot ropes, and the fireman's lift. In the fireman's lift they have to carry another body, with all his equipment, as well as their own, for 200 metres in under 90 seconds. The equipment is in fighting order, weighing about 40 lbs, with a weapon on top of that. You have to rely on your friends. It's nice to know that whoever you're with, he can carry you should the need arise."

By the end of Week 22 they have also completed a 4 mile speed march. This is carried out in fighting order equipment. In speed-marching you run a hundred yards, then walk a hundred yards. In actual fact the speed-marcher runs along the flat and downhill, and walks uphill only. The general speed for that would be about 10 minutes per mile. The nine-miler would be the next phase, at the same speed. The nine-mile speed-march is talked about with awe. Many say it is worse than the ultimate thirty miler. But different recruits respond differently. They are all very much fitter now, no-one carrying a spare ounce of fat, despite permanent mammoth appetites. They say they feel more confident, despite the pain.

"Then they go onto the commando course, which is five weeks long, and that's where everything you've been taught so far, plus other physical aspects, are put into operation. Having passed out on the assault course, they go on to what is termed the Tarzan course. It's a series of obstacles at varying heights from the ground. There are methods and techniques of crossing obstacles or open spaces. We use this to promote confidence, and coordination as well as fitness. After that, they have to do the assault course and the Tarzan course combined.

Battle Fitness Training at Lympstone. Recruits do several consecutive circuits of this assault course during a session, running with basic weapon and equipment, top left, learning to scale and use ropes, below left, climbing structures, above, mounting obstacles, top right, crossing rivers the hard way and displaying general agility, below and right.

RICHARD SCOLLINS · 1985

People are failing all the way through the course. Some of them just don't pass the tests. Often it's not because of lack of physical effort, but through a lack of mental effort. In other words their mind gives in before their body does. All the time we're concerned with the concept of military fitness as opposed to the civilian idea of physical fitness. In military fitness we're talking about not only the physical side of it, but certainly also the emotional fitness, the mental fitness, coupled with the technique that gives you military fitness. That is why they're always kept under stress, to drive them to their limits and bring out the mental and emotional state."

By Week 27, with speed-marcing continuing, the recruits are introduced to the endurance course, an obstacle course out on Woodbury Common, which they have to get round before running back to camp, in full equipment. In all they cover about 6½ miles, within a time limit of ninety minutes. They also have to shoot at the end of that, so throughout the obstacle course weapons must be kept clean and functional. By the end of the course WO2 Scott sees an enormous change in those who have survived the course. They are all immeasureably fitter, but the major change is one of maturity. They are no longer boys.

Mountain and cliff training

The Adventure Training of Week 13 included 'civilian' abseiling, with nylon ropes. In mountain training the recruits and the Mountain Leaders training them use grade-one manila, a hard hemp rope with no stretch in it. Even though the ropes are used for one day only, and then jettisoned, this is cheaper than buying nylon ropes.

Sergeant Gareth Hughes is a Mountain Leader based at Lympstone.

"The recruits come to us at around Week 27 for their first real rope-work.

"The idea is that they come from a boat, to the base of a cliff, and then scale the cliff with a rope. A civilian would climb up the cliff. But for us the rope is a means to an end, to get a body of men up a cliff, and have them up there as quickly as possible. On the recovery the quickest way of clipping a man on is to use a strop, which makes a figure of eight that he steps into, then clip a Karabiner to the strop. When it's time to go down the cliff the rop's passed through the Karabiner, over one of his shoulders, and that's all he has. The rope's grabbed in the right hand and he lowers himself down under control. Everything is in his hands. If he was using civilian equipment the man at the bottom could control it. With this equipment, if he lets go he goes down fast out of control. The way they go down is called a half abseil. In a full abseil you don't use Karabiners, you just wrap the rope round your legs, which we don't teach any more. There are too many injuries from friction burns. They're also taught roller haulage, which is a means of getting stores, or a man

Left: Once trained, the Marine will almost certainly get a Northern Ireland posting – for many, a salutary experience.

carrying stores up a cliff. He's literally pulled up a cliff. We use a 2 in rope and a cliff-head roller, to save wear; a snatch block so that the rope can then be turned at right angles to the cliff."

"In Week 29 we take them for the final phase of their final exercise. They start off in Poole somewhere, they come ashore, do a raid, are helicoptered out, put another raid in, then go on to Plymouth, where they're transferred to boats again, and meet us for the final attack. This is at Port Anthony, in Cornwall. They just abseil on this one. Or, sometimes, use ladders. The main problem is, when they're abseiling for the first time they curl up – they try and get comfort from being close in to the cliff. Whereas in fact they need to push themselves away from it. To be on the safe side you want to be as far away from the cliff as possible. As far as I know, there've been no really serious casualties in training. No safety lines are used. If you get used to a safety line you might not abseil on the day when you haven't got one."

Norway

"Everyone's first winter in Norway is a basic survival, skiing and general military techniques exercise, what they call a Novice Training Period, covering skiing, survival, things like how to erect anything from a brush-wood bivvy up to a ten-man tent. That's the first five weeks. In the second winter they might learn snow and ice techniques, but it's subject to the weather and the availability of kit. The only ones who get a high priority on that are the reconnaissance troops within the unit. These are the advance task force of the unit. The best marines in a commando unit will go forward to a selection committee for recce troop. The SNCOs and corporals in a recce troop are normally Mountain

Below: First year ski-training for 'K' Company, RM, in Norway. The Mountain and Arctic Warfare Cadre specialise in such terrain.

Left: Huddled together for warmth rather than protection from an enemy, Marines on Arctic training wait to be air-lifted out by Sea King helicopter after a night exercise. The climate is an enemy to be feared and respected like a skilled opponent, and learning to live and fight in sub-zero temperatures presents as many new hazards as the jungle.

Leaders. The nucleus of snipers is usually held within the recce troop. They probably would not consider you for a recce troop unless you'd been at least 3 years in a normal rifle company. Men are chosen for being specially good at a number of skills, and they're usually the most enthusiastic marines as well. Those trained for recce are well seasoned marines. They will also be parachute-trained, if not before they join, then after. Within the Corps, the SBS, the Mountain Leaders, and the Recce Troop are the only three groups operationally required to be able to parachute (which is learned at RAF Brize Norton).

The trained MLI will have as a main job running courses in Norway. The basics are taught in the UK before going to Norway. Everyone, 1st year or not, has to attend the pre-Norway lectures. In UK they'd run thru all the shelters. The first lecture might be on the fitting and wearing of Arctic clothing. They've

Above left and right: Before and after. Young trainees arrive willing – in most cases – fit (in fewer) and unco-ordinated in groups of more than one. Right: A King's squad forms up before marching onto the parade square at Lympstone prior to their passing out parade, having just officially received the coveted green beret.

got all this kit and they don't know what its for. Apart from the denims and shirt, everything else is different. There are a number of instructions to give on the care and maintenance and waxing of skis. The really important lectures will be repeated in Norway, things like avalanches, cold weather injuries – frostbite and hypothermia and how to deal with them. Other lectures include Survival and emergencies, mountain safety, selection of campsite, ski-waxing. The 1st week consists of nothing but skiing and mini lectures. In the practical instruction there is as much downhill skiing as possible. Everyone has to learn their winter techniques with a full kit load of 60 lbs plus a weapon – a total of some 75 lbs. To this must be added ammunition when on operations. Novice and continuation training takes up 3 weeks. This is followed by a period of Company tactics to try out the newly acquired or renovated skills. After this

period comes a commando exercise. The 3 months ends up usually with a joint NATO exercise including marines from Holland, the US and Norway.

Passing out
In Week 29 the troop carries out its final big physical test, the 30-mile speed-march. Questioned on the eve of this they all said that they were looking forward to getting it over with. It was the last thing standing between them and the Green Beret. In another week's time they would take part in the King's Squad pass-out parade. Their parents would be present to see them formally receive the Green Berets. No-one seriously entertained the idea of failing this final test. They were not looking forward to it with eagerness. Thirty miles at speed is no picnic. It was just that they all knew that they would complete it. It was not even an ebullient confidence. They had come so far. There was no way they were going to fail now.

The parade would finish. Bedding and equipment on loan would be returned. They would go home on leave, to inspire friends and relatives with their achievement. And more would walk into recruiting offices, do the three pull-ups, and take the train to Lympstone, to be met with the sight of the assault course on the platform.

ONE WHO WAS THERE
40 Commando, RN – Brunei

A hundred marines of 40 Commando went to Brunei for a six-weeks jungle training trip in February 1985. It was the first time many of them had been there. The purpose of the Brunei training was to provide the Commando with a cadre of jungle-trained men. In the course of the six weeks there was one day off. The rest of the time was spent working.

"We learned how to build houses and live in the jungle; what to eat and how to catch it. You caught anything that moves – pigs, monkeys, snakes. I saw a python – it was enormous. It had gone for someone and they'd shot it. We didn't eat it, but if I had to I would. It'd probably be quite nice actually. People go on about snakes, but the worst things I saw out there were the hornets." Other jungle denizens included civet cats, ants, giant scorpions, and mosquitoes. The mosquitoes were a constant problem, particularly during the rare nights spent at the base camp. They seemed impervious to massive drenchings of mosquito repellent, and everyone woke up covered in lumps. The repellent itself caused rashes and rawness.

Training consisted of a series of short exercises, sleeping out for two or three nights at a time, and often having instruction lectures out in the field. Shelters were made from branches, with a raised floor, and a hanging mosquito net. Unlike Cyprus, the heat in the jungles of Brunei is accompanied by a very high level of humidity, which saps the energy and leads to heat exhaustion.

"I find that when it happens to me, the first thing I know is that my legs start tingling. That's when I know I'm going to come down with it. I feel like I'm really working hard, but I'm slowing down. Then I feel a real pressure in my head, and I know something's wrong. It's not painful at all. It's as if you're dreaming, but when you try and focus on things, everything's blurred. You can't hear people. Some people get a dimness of vision, and slurred speech. They think they're talking sense, but they're not.

"To deal with people with heat exhaustion, you have to cool them down. If necessary you have to put them in a stream. You have to stop them smoking, and don't give them salt tablets. Generally its a cas-evac. They've got to be taken out as soon as possible. If you're moving, and it's operational, you can't afford to have someone lagging behind. A helicopter or something has to come for him. If he gets to the stage where he collapses, you have to get him out or he could die."

Gruelling exercise tests skills learnt

At the end of the course all the group's newly acquired skills of hunting, trapping, moving through jungle environments and generally surviving and remaining operational were put to the test in an extended eight-day exercise. Divided into platoons or troops of about thirty men each, the Marines had to find and destroy a 'hostile' group hiding in the hills. This exercise was particularly tough. Dehydration and subsequent heat exhaustion were a major problem. Several men had to be evacuated by helicopter, including some who had come down with debilitating sweat rashes. Each man was carrying a sixty pound pack, plus weapons and ammunition bringing the total to around seventy-five pounds. Long trousers and sleeves were essential because of thorns, and a type of razor grass which could inflict a cut requiring stitches.

The group was inserted into the jungle by helicopter, the first wave absailing in to check out the ground for the rest. The terrain was very hilly. Positions were established, and eventually the 'enemy' was located and destroyed. At the end of the successful exercise, a week later, the men of 40 Commando walked out of the jungle to their transport.

Having survived the very real perils of the jungle, including flash floods and falling trees (the biggest actual killer of personnel), they left Brunei, spending 6 days Rest and Recreation in Hong Kong on the way home. On returning to the UK the group went on to the North of England for exercises. In Brunei the temperature had been as high as 130F, but now they had to face arctic conditions. In the blizzards and winds of a freak wintry spell, with extremely low temperatures, the men who had been in Brunei were more susceptible than most to the danger of hypothermia, and the exercise had to be cancelled for safety reasons.

Left: A Marine of 40 Commando prepares a meal near his 'basher' during jungle training in Brunei.

Below: Marines at the Jungle Warfare School during a patrol exercise. Marines are trained to fight in a variety of environments from the Norwegian arctic to the tropical jungles of Belize and Brunei.

Chapter 3

FUTURE TRENDS: SPACE WARS

As the US commitment to the deployment of weapons in space becomes more clear cut, it is worth while examining something of the history and background to this apparently new phenomenon. Could there be a role for British forces and skills in the military development of Space?

Impression of LTV railgun for the interception and destruction of nuclear armed re-entry vehicles in space.

"Let me share with you a vision of the future that offers hope. It is that we embark on a programme to counter the awesome Soviet missile threat with measures that are defensive. What if free people could live secure in the knowledge that their security did not rest upon the threat of instant US retaliation to deter a Soviet attack, that we could intercept and destroy strategic ballistic missiles before they reach our own soil or that of our allies? I know this is a formidable technical task, one that may not be accomplished before the end of the century. Yet current technology has attained a level of sophistication where it is reasonable for us to begin this effort." Thus began US President Reagan's famous 'Star Wars' speech of 23rd March 1983 in which he offered the American people the populist concept of a space-based defensive umbrella to protect them from a Soviet nuclear missile attack. Now into its third year, the 'strategic defence initiative' (SDI), as the programme is more properly known, continues to generate intense debate as to its viability and widespread fears about its potential effect on the superpower military balance. Most recently, this debate has re-intensified with the issuing of an invitation to America's NATO allies, Israel and Japan, to join in the concept's development.

SDI a product of Western rightism

Despite the press bally-hoo surrounding SDI, more sober analysis shows it to be rather less revolutionary than at first might be imagined. Indeed, it is not too farfetched to describe the present programme as the inevitable outcome of the swing to the right in Western politics combined with the very nature of the superpower nuclear stand-off. Space and most especially that area just beyond the earth's atmosphere has consistently played a part in the nuclear equation since the mid-Fifties when it was realised that intercontinental ballistic missiles (ICBMs) and artifical satellites were a practical proposition. This being the case, it is crucial to the understanding of the SDI concept to be aware of the exo-atmospheric (outside the atmosphere) developments to date.

Within the current structure of world affairs, a balance is struck between the ambitions of the two superpowers, Russia and the US, by means of their ability to destroy each other with nuclear weapons. In both cases, this ability is based on a 'triad' system comprising manned strategic bombers, ground launched ICBMs and missile-armed submarines. Of these elements, the ground- and submarine-launched missiles are potentially the most destructive and their very mode of operation

Right: The submarine-launched element of the Triad system (which with the deployment of SLCMs is more properly called the Quadrad system) is the Trident 1C missile currently carried by *Ohio* class of SSBNs operated by the US Navy. Britain is currently laying down a new generation of T-class submarines to deploy this weapon, the new replacement for the ageing Polaris.

Right: The land-based arm of theTriad system is the MX-1 Peacemaker seen being launched. This ICBM, which can carry up to ten independently targeted nuclear warheads, is now scheduled to be based in hardened silos originally designed for the Minuteman missile system, which it is replacing. Both Trident and MX-1 can qualify as space weapons in that a large part of their trajectory is exo-atmospheric, when they are vulnerable to satellites.

makes them already 'space weapons' in that a percentage of their flight time is spent either very high up in the atmosphere or truly exo-atmospheric.

Space race dominated by military

Equally, the destructive power and speed of delivery of such weapons makes their detection at the earliest possible moment after launch crucial. The ability to put man-made objects into earth orbit opened up hitherto unthinkable possibilities in the fields of reconnaissance and detection over large parts of the earth's surface. Accordingly, both the Soviet and US space programmes have and continue to include a high percentage of purely military missions. Today, optical/electronic reconnaissance and early warning satellites are being joined by increasing numbers of communications, navigation and meteorological platforms to the point where the successful prosecution of warfare is heavily dependent on the availablity of such space-based systems. Some idea of the importance of this area can be gained from the figure of 14,486 man-made objects which are known to have been placed in orbit between the launching of the world's first artificial satellite on 4th October 1957 and the 31st December 1983. Of this number, by far the greatest percentage have belonged to Russia or the US with national totals of 8,998 and 5,150 respectively. Obviously not all these objects have had a military purpose but enough do (some sources suggesting that perhaps half the satellites launched are non-peaceful) to have made counter measures against them continuously attractive to the military technologists on both sides of the ideological divide.

The assault on potentially hostile satellite systems began almost by accident during 1962 when a joint USAF-US Atomic Energy Commission high altitude nuclear test was found to have knocked-out a number of satellites. What was most interesting about this 'Starfish' explosion was that the satellite damage was not inflicted by the blast but by the intense burst of electromagnetic energy which accompanied it. Now known as the 'electro-magnetic pulse' (EMP), this energy surge was found to have a devastating effect on electronic circuitry even at considerable distances from the blast. The effects of the nuclear EMP have over the years been intensively studied and most current military electronic equipment is, to a lesser or greater extent, 'hardened' against it. Back in 1962 however, the phenomenon was a revelation and a timely one in view of the then current American fear that the Russians, with their satellite technology, were about to introduce per-

Above: The Trestle electromagnetic pulse facility at Kirkland Air Force Base, New Mexico, can electronically simulate the electro-magnetic effects of a nuclear detonation on an aircraft's avionics. A B52 bomber has been towed up the ramp onto the 200ft high trestle to test its electrical components.

manently orbiting nuclear bombs. In view of these factors, President Kennedy authorised an anti-satellite (ASAT) programme based on the EMP effect which resulted in the creation of the 'Squanto Terror' ASAT test station on Johnson Island in the Pacific.

The 'Squanto Terror' programme continued until 1968 when it was cancelled following the ratification of an international treaty banning the use of nuclear weapons in space. Ironically, as this first American essay into space warfare wound down, the Russians began their own ASAT programme. Mindful of the same treaty which had ended 'Squanto Terror', the Soviets concentrated on the development of a system which used conventional explosives to destroy a target. The first Russian ASAT test took place during October 1968 and consisted of manoeuvring a vehicle into an attack position rather than a full blown exercise culminating in an explosion. The first detonations in the programme occurred during the period 20th to 30th October 1970 when Cosmos 374 exploded close to the previously launched Cosmos 373 on the 23rd of the month. A week later, Cosmos 375 repeated the exercise.

Soviets score in low orbits

By the end of 1971, the Soviet Union had made 12 ASAT 'interceptions' and was regarded in the West as having proved its ability to attack and destroy satellites in low earth orbits. This ability was further demonstrated on 3rd December 1971 when Cosmos 462 succeeded in destroying a 'target' at an altitude of only 257km. Probably because of the then current strategic arms limitation talks (SALT), Russian ASAT tests were discontinued until February 1976 and the launch of Cosmos 803. The general capability was further refined with the launching of Cosmos 1174 during April 1980 which made three passes at a 'target', Cosmos 1171, and lead to considerable speculation as to whether or not it was evaluating a laser weapon or sighting system.

Above: Sprint and Spartan missiles of the now defunct US Safeguard anti-ballistic system positioned ready for launch.

A further test vehicle, Cosmos 1243, was launched on 2nd February 1981 and showed itself capable of independent manouevres in order to increase the chances of a 'kill'. At this point, the Americans announced their belief that the Russian 'killer sats' were an operational system rather than an experimental programme using manouevrable hardware which destroyed its target by blasting it with a shotgun-like spread of pellets.

Returning to the point where 'Squanto Terror' was cancelled, the US was also deeply involved in an 'anti-ballistic missile' (ABM) programme aimed at producing a ground-based system which could knock out ballistic missiles as they re-entered the earth's atmosphere. As early as June 1955, the US Army awarded contracts to both Western Electric and Bell for studies of a guided missile defence system for use against ICBMs. By the end of the following year, this work led to the initiation of the Nike-Zeus programme with the first such round being fired some three years later in August 1959. After

the initial proving trials, Nike-Zeus made its first successful interception of an ICBM over the Kwajalein range in the Pacific during June 1962.

Enter Sentinel – the starting point

With the ABM concept thus proven, the Nike-Zeus programme was modified to include a second weapon, Sprint, and an advanced radar acquisition system. Now known as Nike-X, the programme reached a major way point in June 1964 when the first of these radars began tests at the White Sands missile range in the SW of America. This milestone was followed by the first launch of a Sprint round in November 1965 which in turn paved the way for the multi-billion dollar 'Sentinel' ABM system to be authorised during September 1967. Within the technical limitations of its day, the 'Sentinel' system may be considered as the forerunner of today's SDI concept, being intended to provide a comprehensive defence umbrella for both civilian and military targets in the continental USA.

For various reasons, 'Sentinel' proved to be too ambitious and in March 1969, it was superseded by the

'Safeguard' system. 'Safeguard', using the existing Sprint weapon and a new missile named Spartan for exo-atmospheric interceptions, was intended to protect the USAF's ICBM silos only. In August 1969, the Senate approved the deployment of the system at Malmstrom AFB in Montana and Grand Forks AFB in North Dakota. Work on the Spartan segment of the system had actually begun in 1965 with the first launch of the weapon being made in 1968. The 'Safeguard' go-ahead accelerated work on Spartan which in the event, made its first ICBM 'kill' (on 28th August 1970) before similar confirmation of Sprint's ability in this direction. The technological difficulties inherent in Sprint's role as a short range 'last chance' weapon probably contributed to its lengthy gestation but by the end of 1970, it in turn had destroyed an incoming ICBM during a test on the 23rd of December.

'Safeguard' proceeded apace with additional launch complexes being planned for Whiteman AFB in Missouri and Warren AFB in Wyoming until May 1972, when President Nixon signed the USA/USSR ABM

Left: Sprint surface-to-air high-acceleration missile being launched from Kwajalein atoll in the Pacific during early tests of the system. Sprint was the short-range interceptor missile in the system, armed with a nuclear warhead for the detonation of incoming missile. Below: PAR (Perimeter Acquisition Radar) of the Safeguard system in North Dakota.

treaty which limited ABM deployment on both sides to 100 missiles sited around their respective capital cities and at one other location. On 27th May 1972, work on the Malstrom complex was stopped and the planned locations at Whiteman and Warren were scrapped. This left only the Grand Forks segment of the original system and in April 1975, what remained of 'Safeguard' achieved its initial operational capability with 28 Sprint and 8 Spartan missiles at this site. During the preceding test programme, 54 Sprint and Spartan missiles had been fired (including a Sprint test against a submarine-type missile on 7th May 1971), of which 47 were adjudged to have been completely successful.

Safeguard abandoned at peak

Despite the fact that 'Safeguard' worked, the system only survived until October 1975 when the US decided to put out of the operational ABM game, concentrating instead on the continuance of development programmes for future systems should they be needed, a philosophy which has carried through into the Eighties. Having undertaken such an expensive 20 year long development programme, one cannot be blamed for wondering why 'Safeguard' should have been abandonded just at the point where it had become an operational reality. Obviously, the 1972 ABM treaty had a profound effect along with the staggering cost of the enterprise. Equally, the provision of a single ABM complex only invali-

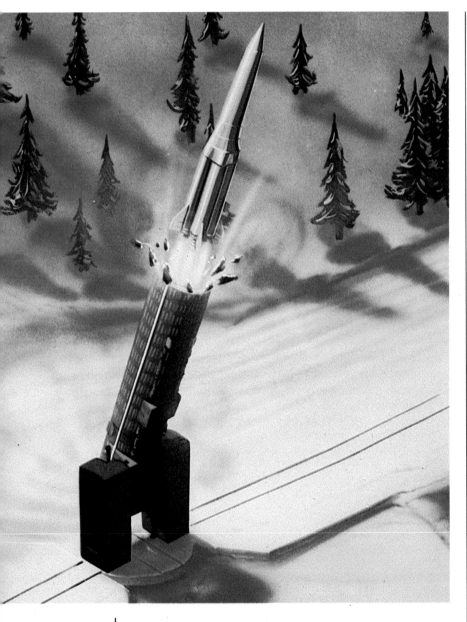

Above: Artist's impression of Soviet Galosh anti-ballistic missile interceptor as used to defend Moscow. It is believed to be similar to the US Spartan weapon. Right: Diagram showing the different types of missile and missile-interceptor likely to confront one another in space.

dated the original concept in that 'Safeguard' was intended to protect enough American ICBM launch sites to make a credible retaliatory strike against a Soviet attack. Protection for one missile base hardly represented any sort of response, let alone a credible one, to such a situation. More subtly however, there were some in the Senate who were not sorry to see the back of 'Safeguard'. Right from the very beginning of the programme there were those who considered the whole 'Sentinel'/'Safeguard' concept dangerously destabilising to the delicate balance of nuclear deterrence between Russia and America. Indeed, Senate approval for the 'Safeguard' system had been gained by a margin of one vote back in 1969 because of just such concerns.

Equally, both Sprint and Spartan were themselves nuclear weapons and there was considerable fears that in the act of destroying the incoming missiles, their nuclear warheads might do as much damage as the weapons they were intended to stop. It is interesting to note that in the political climate of the mid-Sixties and the Seventies, the fear of destabilising the world order was enough to check if not stop the introduction of systems like 'Safeguard'. The same arguments are being raised today concerning SDI but the chances of caution prevailing over confrontation are slim with the current swing away from an East-West dialogue.

Soviet go-slow on Galosh

The American abandonment of operational ABMs was not matched by the Soviet Union. The Russians unveiled their system, known in the West as 'Galosh', for the first time in 1964. Considered by the Pentagon to be a similar weapon to Spartan (an exo-atmospheric interceptor), in fact, very little is known about 'Galosh's' potential other than that it is operational and is deployed around Moscow in four complexes each armed with 16 missiles. This gives a total figure of 64 rounds against the treaty ceiling of 100 and the Russians have so far shown no inclination to exceed this agreed figure. Indeed, during 1968, it was quite widely believed that a pronounced slowdown in the weapon's deployment was attributable to a Soviet abandonment of the concept. This is now seen not to be the case but rather a readjustment of the system to cope with the threat provided by the newly introduced Chinese ICBM capability and the possible replacement of existing rounds with an improved variant.

By 1979/80, the Americans had become convinced that the Soviets had two new ABMs under development and that one or other of them would replace 32 of the existing 'Galosh' weapons in the near term. The assessment also saw the start of a string of American claims that Russia was in violation of the 1972 treaty which continue to the present day. Current US thinking on the subject as summarised in the "Soviet Military Power 1985" handbook, suggests that the Moscow ABM system is being developed into a two layer defence using new tracking and guidance radars, ABM-1B 'Improved Galosh' missiles and a new silo-based, high acceleration weapon to counter the ICBMs the 'Galosh's' miss. The handbook goes on to indicate that the conventional SA-10 and SA-X-12 surface-to-air missiles "may have the potential to intercept some types of US strategic ballistic missile."

US Space missile ready for deployment

In the light of current Soviet ASAT developments, it is hardly surprising that the US has re-entered the field with an air-launched weapon developed by a consortium of Vought, Boeing and McDonnell-Douglas. Work on this latest ASAT began during the Seventies and a three-stage weapon is already under test and set for

Star Wars

USA

USSR

1	**US Early Warning Satellite**	**6**	**Air-launched ASAT (from F-15)**
2	**USSR 'Killer Satellite'**	**7**	**US homing overlay impact weapon**
3	**US Battlestation (laser-particle beam)**	**8**	**Shuttle servicing battlestation**
4	**MIRV's (Multiple Independently-targeted Re-entry Vehicles)**	**9**	**Soviet ICBMs (InterContinental Ballistic Missiles)**
5	**Satellite reflecting ground-based laser**		

10	**Missile silo**
11	**Medium-range ground-based laser/particle beam weapon defending missile silos**
12	**Long-range ground-based laser weapon**

operational deployment in the near future. The launch vehicle is a modified F-15 Eagle fighter aircraft which carries specialised launch equipment in its weapons bay, the missile itself on a ventral rack, new guidance and launch software in its onboard computer and a modified pilot's head-up display providing steering cues for weapons launch. The ASAT itself comprises a modified Boeing SRAM missile as its first stage, a Vought Altair III second stage and a 'miniature' warhead as its third stage. The method of operation appears to be a launch phase in which the carrier aircraft enters a zoom-climb, a boost phase in which the first and second stage rockets propel the vehicle into space and a terminal 'kill' phase in which the warhead homes in on the target. The exact nature of this last segment is not at all clear, with no details of the guidance system or type of warhead used having yet been released. What is more certain is that the USAF intends to deploy the weapon as soon as possible with the F-15 – equipped 318th Fighter Interceptor Squadron (FIS) at McChord AFB, Washington, and the 48th FIS at Langley AFB, Virginia already slated to receive the weapon.

With such a background, Reagan's 'Star Wars' programme can be placed in its proper perspective, a resurgence of interest in ABM and ASAT systems based on a foundation of a series of programmes stretching back into the Fifties. What marks SDI out is its return

Top left: Artist's impression of the Soviet SA-10 surface-to-air missile system. Left: Impression of the Soviet SA-X-12 surface-to-air missile system with associated tracker, reload, fire-control and support vehicles deployed to fire. Below: Preparing to load an ASAT (anti-satellite missile) onto an F-15 Eagle during trials at the Boeing Development Center. The missile is launched into the atmosphere and then climbs away into space to find its target.

to the concept of an umbrella defence first set out in the abandoned 'Sentinel' programme of the late Sixties; the technological ability to take at least part of the proposed system permanently into space and, most importantly, the use of direct energy weapons.

Particle beam weapons

Even these futuristic weapons have a considerable background in US weapons technology dating back to the Sixties when the theoretical possibilities of the concentrated light beam, or laser, and the directed flow of high energy particles making-up a partical beam as weapons were first appreciated. As early as 1960, the US had investigated the particle-beam weapons field under the project name 'See Saw'. Several years of experimentation yielded only limited success and produced the conclusion that such a weapon was possible but decades away from even a test example, let alone an operational system. In the light of this, it came as a considerable surprise to the American intelligence community when it was discovered in the early Seventies that the Russians appeared not only to be experimenting in the field but doing so with every sign of success.

The physical theory behind the partical beam is complex in the extreme but at its simplest involves giving electrons, protons or ions enormous energy by accelerating them by means of an electrical field. To do this, what is known as a linear or cyclotron accelerator is needed requiring staggering amounts of electrical power to drive it. Indeed, it was the sheer size of the necessary accelerator and its power requirements which convinced the Americans in the Sixties that such a weapon was presently impractical. Once the acceleration process has taken place and the beam has been

concentrated through 'lenses', its constituent subatomic particles are travelling at speeds close to that of light. When they are confronted with the molecular structure of an obstacle in their path, they generate heat to the point where the obstacle vaporises or disintegrates. It is believed that this effect is true for all known substances, hence the attractions of the particle beam as a weapon.

Are Soviets ahead with particle beam weapon?

Returning to the Russian work in the field, US reconnaissance satellites began to produce evidence in the early Seventies of some very strange developments at the Azgir test area near Semipalatinsk in Central Russia. As the available data increased, it was concluded that the Azgir site contained, amongst other things, a 213m long linear accelerator and accompanying underground fusion generators to provide the necessary electrical power (a fusion generator is essentially a controlled nuclear explosion from which electricity is tapped directly). At first, going by their own experience, American experts dismissed the idea, ascribing a range of other uses to the Azgir structure. In 1976 however, an early warning satellite orbiting over the Indian Ocean picked up the unmistakable emissions from a fusion generator which could only be located at Azgir. Such indications continued and in the late Seventies a further complex at Sarova near Gorki was firmly identified as being a test site for a particle beam-type ABM weapon.

After considerable and acrimonious debate between the USAF intelligence agencies and the CIA, it was

Below: Artwork cutaway of the White Horse accelerator test stand at US National Laboratory at Los Alamos, part of US experimentation in the development of particle beam weapons.

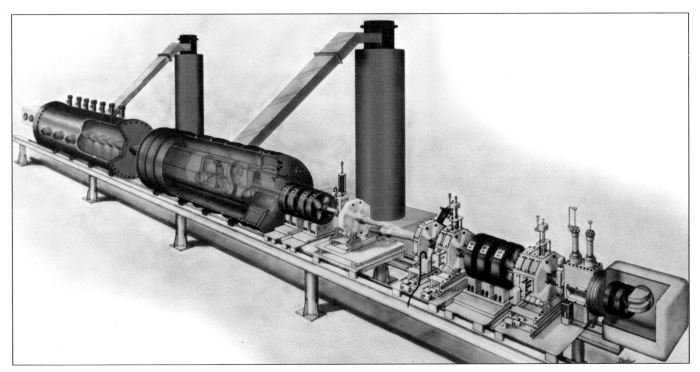

Above: Impression of a Soviet orbital anti-satellite weapon. Like a space shotgun, it is firing a stream of shot-like fragments at the enemy satellite.

finally accepted that the Russians were working on practical direct energy weapons. Even then, the newly elected President Carter stated that he could see no prospect for such weapons in the near future by the Soviet Union and it was only in late 1978 that a serious programme to look into the field was re-established.

With most of the building blocks now in place, America started down the road to SDI. The maintenance of a continuing ABM technology programme together with the work being done on direct energy weapons gave the necessary scientific foundation whilst genuine fears about the Soviet Union's ASAT, ABM and energy weapons provided some of the political will. The final catalyst in the process was the election of President Reagan in 1980. After two decades which had seen the disgrace of one President and the failure of another's policy of detente, America was ready for strong leadership and a return to the 'Golden Age' of the Fifties when the US had undisputed superiority over the Soviet Union. Reagan was the man of the moment and his simplistic view of America's place in the world (out in front) won him a landslide victory. Thus established, he set America's political face firmly to the right and provided

an administration which gave the 'hawks' the chance they had been waiting for. The military budget mushroomed, America re-armed frightningly quickly and the old umbrella defence concept was dusted down and stirringly packaged as a clarion call to the country's technological excellence in the President's 'Star Wars' speech of March 1983.

As originally conceived, SDI sets out to provide the US with a multi-layered ABM and ASAT defence in the short and medium term. The cornerstone of the system will be space-based energy weapons designed to knock out Soviet ICBMs in the first five minutes of their flight when they are at their most vulnerable. Currently work in this area is concentrated on the 'Excalibur' nuclear-pumped X-ray laser and the 'White Horse' particle beam system. 'Excalibur', developed by the Lawrence Livermore Laboratory in San Fransico, seems to offer the best hope of a laser system compact enough and producing a stable enough beam to be of use in an operational system. Work with conventional chemical lasers suggests that they would be simply too large to deploy easily in space and at the power levels required, suffer from a phenomena known as 'jitter' in which the beam cannot be focused on a particular area of a target for any length of time. The 'Excalibur' system must be regarded as a medium to long term development and there is parallel consideration taking place of refined,

Above: Impression of US anti-satellite system using a rotating mirror for targeting a laser weapon. Tests with ground-based lasers are currently using the space shuttle as a target.

ground based chemical lasers which would use space-based 'mirrors' to focus their beams on to a target. The size factor would not be a problem in such systems and they would offer an operational capability at a much earlier date. Currently, preparations are being made to test the aim of chemical lasers from ground stations using the Shuttle as a target.

Space Shuttle to service space armoury

Mention of the Space Shuttle provides the opportunity to note its significance to the overall SDI concept. Bearing in mind that the vehicle has always been intended for both military and civilian use, it will be the Shuttle which will take the major load in delivering the energy weapons into orbit and the means by which they will be serviced once deployed. As presently used, the Shuttle design is a compromise between military and scientific needs and the USAF would certainly like to see a greater lift capacity than it is currently capable of. With the establishment of SDI, there is increasing talk of a 'Block II' Shuttle which would be tailored specifically to the needs of the military for use in the late 1990s. Whether such a development will materialise remains to be seen.

The value of re-usable space vehicles has not been lost on the world outside the US and currently the Soviets are testing such a vehicle whilst Britain, France and Japan all have projected vehicles though it seems unlikely that the European and Japanese vehicles, if they are even built, would have any role in SDI. Equally, the prospect of US-Soviet Shuttle battles which have been mooted in certain press reports seem to belong to science fiction rather than sober analysis.

Like 'Excalibur', the 'White Horse' particle beam system, under development at Los Alamos in New Mexico, must also be a medium to long term development, despite reports of elements of the system being tested in the 1986-87 time scale. As currently envisaged, a 'White Horse' 'battlestar' will weigh about as much as a fully loaded F-15 fighter (30,845kg), putting it just within the current payload capacity of the Shuttle (29,485kg). Stationed in low earth orbit, between 10 and 40 such platforms are considered to offer an effective operational capability. As far as is known, 'White Horse' will use sub-atomic particles of Hydrogen to make up its energy beam and will be used against ICBMs in their 'boost' (take-off) and 'mid-course' (exo-atmospheric trajectory) phases.

Such weapons will require space-based back up in the form of an extensive network of early warning satellites to alert the system to missile launches. From the fore-

going, it will be seen that this exo-atmospheric segment of the SDI concept will require enormous effort to achieve and is not likely to be seen even in an interim form much before the end of this century.

Ground-based elements already established

Much nearer in time are the various ground based measures which will complement the space elements of the system. As already noted, ground based chemical lasers are already under development and similarly sited particle beam weapons are in the pipeline. Both forms of installation would form excellent counters to those ICBMs which will inevitably slip through the 'high frontier' line of defence. Again, the air launched ASAT is already well into its development programme and will offer the USAF a flexible counter to Soviet 'killersats' attempting to destroy the 'battlestars' and their attendant early warning platforms. Equal hope in this direction is offered by the 'homing overlay' ASAT which was successfully tested during early 1984. The weapon uses conventional rocketry to boost it into space where it deploys an inert but guided 'warhead' which destroys its target by the simple expedient of crashing into it. As a final 'last chance' element to the system, conventional missiles like the Sprint system are again under consideration, the whole package offering the glittering prospect of a defence capable of dealing with attacking ICBMs from launch to terminal dive.

Despite the nearly 30 years of ground work behind SDI, the technological hurdles to be overcome remain enormous, especially in the area of controlling the system. Under the still-adhered to SALT II treaty, Russia and the US are allowed 1,200 missiles with multiple warheads. When it is considered that most current weapons can carry as many as ten separate warheads, it will be realised that the SDI system could be theoretically confronted with as many as 12,000 separate targets at the present time! Whilst obviously, SDI's aim is to destroy as many missiles as possible before they deploy their warheads, the targeting problem still remains enormous, a situation which will be exacerbated almost certainly by the use of decoys designed to confuse the system. Controlling SDI will require software of unparalleled complexity and probably the development of a new generation of supercomputers which, some have suggested, may have to incorporate a degree of independent 'intelligence' outside their programming to cope with the work load. Allied to this are the necessary developments required to produce suitable tracking and guidance radars together with optical, infra-red and laser sighting and homing systems for the ASATs. Indeed the technological effort required to create a suitable command and control system for the concept is perhaps greater than that necessary to produce

Left: US Army HOE missile lifts off from the Kwajalein Missile Range pad on Meck island for the US's first direct-intercept of an ICBM re-entry vehicle in June 1984.

the weapons themselves. It is little wonder therefore that the Defensive Technologies Study Team which reported on SDI to President Reagan in 1983 proposed that half the $15 billion budget set aside for the programme should be used to develop the necessary command, control and communications structure.

Almost inevitably, this original cost figure has risen dramatically, standing currently at $26 billion over a five to six year period. Equally, the aims of the concept have been modified with the passage of time. As now envisaged, there is a possibility of an interim SDI capability being introduced to defend US ICBM silos whilst the ultimate goal of a total umbrella is worked through. The concept of a total defence still appears to remain at the core of the programme but there are doubts being expressed about the time span necessary to achieve such an end.

Repercussions and reverberations among Superpower allies and opponents

Predictably, the Soviet Union has reacted violently to SDI, seeing it as an offensive rather than a defensive measure designed to give the US military superiority and as a major if not irrevocable block to any genuine negotiated arms reduction. Perhaps more surprisingly, the SDI proposal has received a very cool reception from America's NATO allies including the UK whose present government can usually be relied on by Washington to tow the US line. European worries over SDI take a number of forms ranging from the effects it will have on attempts to reduce the nuclear stock pile to a simple disbelief in the schemes' viability. Within this spectrum, a major European worry is that SDI could easily lead to a return to American isolationism, leaving the rest of NATO in disarray without the American nuclear shield upon which it now relies for its credibility. The viability point was neatly summed up by Foreign Secretary Howe when in a 1985 speech, he warned of the dangers of trying to create a 'Maginot Line' in space.

The European dilemma has been further exacerbated by the American invitation to its NATO partners together with Israel and Japan, to become involved in the SDI development programme. This has generated much heart-searching because of the fears existent about SDI's consequences when weighed against the industrial benefits that might be gained from participation. Equally, the American plan to extend SDI cover to Europe incorporated in the invitation is widely seen as being even less effective than the American cover. Within Europe, Denmark, Norway and Greece have already turned the offer down, with only the UK and West Germany showing any real interest, which, in the latter case, already appears to be waning. The waters have been further muddied by France who has proposed a counter European-based high tech collaboration under the title 'Eureka'. The 'Eureka' programme is based on fears that the proposed SDI technological 'two-way street' will turn out to be as all other US-Europe collaborations appear to have been, distinctly 'one-way' in America's favour. This reticence has been deepended by the discovery that participation in SDI will not, as was at first thought, mean a slice of the $26 bn research budget but rather nationally funded work.

The UK has taken a leading role in this debate and is currently backing both SDI and 'Eureka'. The Thatcher government's stance is that SDI should be developed but not deployed, being used rather as a bargaining chip in the arms reduction process.

A role for Britain

If the UK does participate in SDI, industrial analysts have identified three major areas in which British companies could have a role; namely in the devlopment of 'conventional' missiles for use in the programme's initial stages, in management systems and in software technology. Taking these in order, British Aerospace, Marconi and Hunting Engineering all have experience in the design and development of missiles and their guidance systems. In the field of battle management, Plessey, Marconi and Racal have all produced computer hardware of a suitable type which is already in use throughout NATO. British companies are equally strong, if not stronger, in software design with Software Sciences (part of Thorn-EMI) CAP, Logica, Systems Designers and Scicon (part of BP) all having experience of complex military systems.

Opinion inside industry is divided about the pros and cons of participation with some voicing the fear that the US is unlikely to place direct contracts outside the domestic industry for fear of the technology involved finding its way to Moscow. Others take the view that the technical expertise available in the UK will overcome such American reticence on the grounds that they "need our brains to make it work", whilst a third school of thought suggests tie-ups with the American giants such as Lockheed, Rockwell, TRW and Hughes in the hope of gaining sub-contract work.

That SDI can be made to work in one form or another is beyond question. What is far less clear is whether or not it should be proceeded with, how effective it would be in the face of the inevitable Soviet attempts to counter it and whether or not the European nations should involve themselves with it. There are powerful arguments against its deployment not the least of which is that it will certainly provoke the development of a parallel Soviet system which in turn would lead to the permanent expansion of the superpower confrontation into space, a situation which mankind has so far avoided. Equally importantly, its development will probably put an end to any effective arms limitations agreement between East and West for the foreseeable future. Sadly, such arguments seem to have little effect currently in Washington with an administration which seems have little intention of reaching any kind of understanding with the Soviet Union.

Chapter 4

REGIMENT IN REVIEW: GURKHAS

Born and bred in the distant Himalayan mountains of Nepal, the Gurkhas have become an integral part of British military heritage and tradition. Now these faithful servants of a benign foreign power face the threat of being seen as too anachronistic for modern military needs.

Gurkhas on a landing craft prepare to go ashore during training. They are traditionally wary of water.

The men of the 7th Duke of Edinburgh's Own Gurkha Rifles had a frustrating time during the Falklands Conflict. Wherever they appeared the Argentines surrendered, even when they were entrenched in strong positions. Such is the fearsome reputation of these small brown men from the mountains of Nepal that they can win battles simply by letting it be known that they have arrived on the field. Terrible stories had spread among the Argentine soldiers about what the Gurkhas would do to them with their kukris and when the Argentines heard the war cry of "Ayo Gurkhali" they decided that discretion was indeed the better part of valour.

This reputation seems almost misplaced when visiting the Gurkha lines at Church Crookham near Aldershot. The gate, manned by one unarmed sentry is at the top of an avenue of horse chestnut trees and the barracks has a decidedly old-fashioned look to it. It consists of large wooden huts now so out of date that the Royal

Marines have kept one of them at their modern Commando Training Centre just to show recruits how rough life was in the old army. The Gurkhas, unused to modern amenities, do not complain but go about the business they love most of all; soldiering. There is far more "bull" in a Gurkha barracks than in other regiments in the British army. It is not imposed on them, they actually enjoy spit and polish. Their saluting is punctilious and each salute is returned equally correctly by their officers. Naturally courteous, their behaviour outside the barracks is impeccable and there is a stream of invitations for them, especially their band, to attend all sorts of functions.

Here, in Hampshire, they seem unlikely candidates for the title of the most feared soldiers in the world. But it is the other side of their nature which brought about their unique association with the British army, the side of their motto: "Kafar hunme bhanda morno ramro"– "Better to die than be a coward".

Honourable East Indians face Gorkhas, 1814

The association started in 1814 when the army of the Honourable East India Company marched into Nepal to punish the Nepalese for a series of raids on British frontier posts. With a force of over 40,000 British and Indian troops, 60 guns, more than 1,000 elephants and some 4,000 camels, the Governor General, the Earl of Moira, thought that it would all be over in a couple of months and that he would soon be sitting in Katmandu. But he had reckoned without the martial spirit of the Gurkhas who take their name from the small Principality of Gorkha whose ruler had conquered most of Nepal in the mid-eighteenth century. They had, moreover, the benefit of being trained by deserters from the British army who had taken refuge in Katmandu.

The two armies clashed and almost immediately there appeared the respect for each other which has since characterised the relationship between British and Gurkha soldiers. One British officer, describing the Gurkhas, later wrote: "I never saw more steadiness or bravery exhibited by any set of men in my life. Run they would not and of death they seemed to have no fear, though their comrades were falling thick around them."

It was here that the British first met the kukri, the curved short sword of the Gurkhas. It is in fact a tool for all purposes, being used to harvest crops, cut wood, peel vegetables, slaughter goats and kill enemies. It is kept razor sharp and has a notch near the handle designed to catch an opponents blade and, with a twist, disarm him.

"We could serve under men like you"

Faced by men armed with these weapons, a group of irregulars led by Lieutenant Frederick Young ran away

Left: Men of the 7th Duke of Edinburgh Gurkhas parade through the Hampshire town of Fleet after their return from the Falklands War in 1982. Their reputation did much to weaken Argentine resolve.

Above: Jubilant Gurkhas pose for the camera with a captured 20mm Argentine Oerlikon gun on the Falkland Islands during Operation Corporate. The gun is now deployed in the UK.

in terror. Young stood his ground and the story is told that when the Gurkhas asked him: "But why did you not run away too?" Young replied: "I have not come so far in order to run away. I came to stop." He then calmly sat down to await his fate. But instead of killing him the Gurkha commander said: "We could serve under men like you."

In captivity, Young learnt Gurkhali – a form of Sanskrit – and grew to admire his captors. When he was released he was, in turn, put in charge of Gurkha prisoners and from them in September 1815 he formed the Sirmoor Battalion which is now the 2nd King Edward VII's Own Goorkhas (The Sirmoor Rifles). It is the only regiment which claims the privilege of using the old spelling of Goorkha and it is the Second Battalion of this regiment which is now based at Church Crookham.

The far-sighted as well as courageous Lieutenant Young – he ended his career as a General – is looked upon with great respect today as the founder of the Gurkha Regiments in the British Army.

The war with Nepal ended with an honourable peace in 1816 and the Gurkhas, formed into several battalions, settled down to serve with the British and fought their first battle a year later at Sambhar in the Pindaree War. They performed so well that they were accorded the honour of escorting 300 captured and surrendered guns to Delhi. From then on they were employed in a series of frontier wars and expeditions, fighting and dying for the British.

Loyalty tested by Indian Mutiny

But it was not until the outbreak of the Indian Mutiny that their loyalty was fully appreciated. The Sirmoor Battalion under the Command of Major Charles Reid marched out of their base at Dehra Dun just four hours after a camel trooper brought the first news of the Mutiny. It took them nearly a month of fighting to reach Delhi. There they held a house belonging to a nobleman called Hindu Rao. It was the key to the British position, and alongside them fought the 60th Rifles, now the 2nd Royal Greenjackets, who were so impressed by the fighting hillmen that they later asked that they should be allowed to "conform their dress to that of the 60th and that their sepoys should in future be known as riflemen."

The Sirmoor Battalion held Hindu Rao's House for three months and eight days. They defeated twenty six major attacks, launched three attacks themselves and, reinforced by the Kumoan Battalion (later the 3rd Queen Alexandra's Own Gurkha Rifles), led the storm-

ing of the city in loyal support of the Empire.

When the fighting was over the Sirmoor Battalion had lost eight of its nine officers and 327 of its 490 men had been killed or wounded. Grievous losses, but the Gurkhas had won their unique position in the British army, acknowledged by the British soldiers as their equals.

For the next 57 years, owing allegiance to Queen Victoria as well as their own King, they fought for the British Crown in Afghanistan where even the Pathans feared them, in the frozen mountains of Tibet, in the Burmese jungle and in innumerable frontier skirmishes. Then in 1914 came the Great War. As news of the war filtered through the mountains of Nepal the Gurkhas, unbidden, set out to join their regiments while the Prime Minister of Nepal, Sir Chandra Shamser offered the King Emperor, King George V, "the whole military resources of Nepal". He also arranged religious dispensation for his Hindu soldiers to cross the Kala Pani, the big sea.

World War I

Forming part of the Indian Corps, they were thrown into the line on the Western Front and, although almost drowning in the trench mud, adapted themselves to an entirely different type of warfare. Neuve-Chapelle was their particular battle-ground and in November 1985 a

Above: Gurkhas wielding their Kukris fight alongside men of the 31st Regiment of Foot at the Battle of Sabraon on the 10th of February 1846 during the Sikh Wars. Such events proved their reputation for courage and loyalty.

party of the 2nd Goorkhas visited the battlefield to commemorate the 70th Anniversary of the battle and the many men who died there. It was in France that the Gurkhas won their first VC. Until 1911 they, along with the other "native" regiments of the Indian Army, could win only the VC's Indian equivalent, the Indian Order of Merit but when King George visited Nepal he ordered that from that date Gurkhas would be eligible for the Victoria Cross. The first was awarded to Rifleman Kulbir Thapa of the 2nd Battalion of the 3rd Gurkhas, sole survivor of an attacking force which had been caught on uncut barbed wire and mown down by machine gun fire. Although wounded himself Kulbir brought back two wounded comrades from the barbed wire and then carried a wounded private of the Leicestershire Regiment on his back to safety under heavy German fire. In all the Gurkhas have won 26 Victoria Crosses.

The Gurkhas suffered heavily in the Great War. A battalion of the 8th Gurkhas was wiped out at Loos, fighting to the last man. The 6th Gurkhas won immortal fame at Gallipoli in capturing Gurkha Bluff after a bloody

Above: Sergeant of the 2nd Battalion, 1st Gurkha Rifles during World War 1. Special dispensation was required for the men to cross the sea without breaking religious rules. Right: Gurkha Rifleman at the turn of the century, fully equipped as a British soldier. As regulars in the Indian Army, the Gurkhas owed allegiance to both the British sovereign and their own king.

kukri battle with the Turks. The 2nd Battalion of the 7th Gurkhas suffered through the siege of Kut-Al-Amara in Mesopotamia and the horror of the captivity which followed it. The Gurkhas were so stoical in their captivity that they shamed the Turks into improving their conditions. Some 200,000 Gurkhas fought for Britain in the Great War. Twenty thousand of them died.

The war over, they went back to peace-time soldiering which for the 1st Battalion of the 2nd Goorkhas entailed fighting the Bolsheviks in the Caucasus and North Iran. This battalion returned to its base at Dehra in June 1921 after nearly six years of active service. Other units fought in the third Afghan war and took part in campaigns on the North-West Frontier. And then, when World War II broke out, they once again sailed across the Kala Pani to fight for Britain. No fewer than 40 battalions fought from Syria through the Western Desert to Italy and Greece, in Malaya and Singapore, from Siam in the retreat to Imphal and then in the great adv-

Above: British and native officers of the 1st Gurkhas outside their farmhouse Headquarters during the First World War. Right: Diagram showing the structure of the Brigade of Gurkhas.

ance to Rangoon, during the Burma campaign.

The author John Masters served with the 4th Gurkhas and in his book "The Road Past Mandalay" he wrote: "Of Gurkhas what can I say that will compress the knowledge of fourteen years, and all the love and admiration it gave me, into a few sentences? Their homeland Nepal, the small country sandwiched along the Himalayas between India and Tibet. They are of Mongol extraction; small and sturdy in stature; mountain men all; endowed with an inborn honesty towards life that gives them perfect self-confidence, without any need of swashbuckling or boasting; as fond of pranks as of discipline; cheerful under the worst conditions – especially under the worst conditions; brave, courteous . . ."

World War II

They behaved in the second war as they had in the first. The unfortunate 2nd Battalion of the 7th Gurkhas was captured once again, this time by the Germans at Tobruk in the Western Desert.

Others, captured in the Far East, suffered the most appalling treatment from the Japanese without complaint until even the Japanese grew to admire them. And the Germans had the same fear of them acquired by their fathers in France in WWI.

Brigadier "Birdy" Smith, then a junior officer, has told the story of what happened when the Gurkhas were ordered to take the heavily defended village of Tavoleto, a dominant point in the Gothic Line of defences in Italy. They took a terrible pounding from German mortars and machine guns, no food came up to them, their telephone link was cut and the Germans introduced a Hindustani speaker into their radio net.

The situation was so bad that even the Gurkhas hesitated about going forward. In desperation Smith reminded them of their own saying: "It is better to die than be a coward", and he threatened to go forward alone with his orderly. "The effect", he wrote, "was electrifying, as if I had touched open nerves to unleash the pent-up fear frustration, anger, all compounded by hunger and a dire lack of sleep.

"Jemadar (Platoon commander) Jitbahader Rai of 9th Platoon shrieked 'Ayo Gurkhali', the war cry was repe-

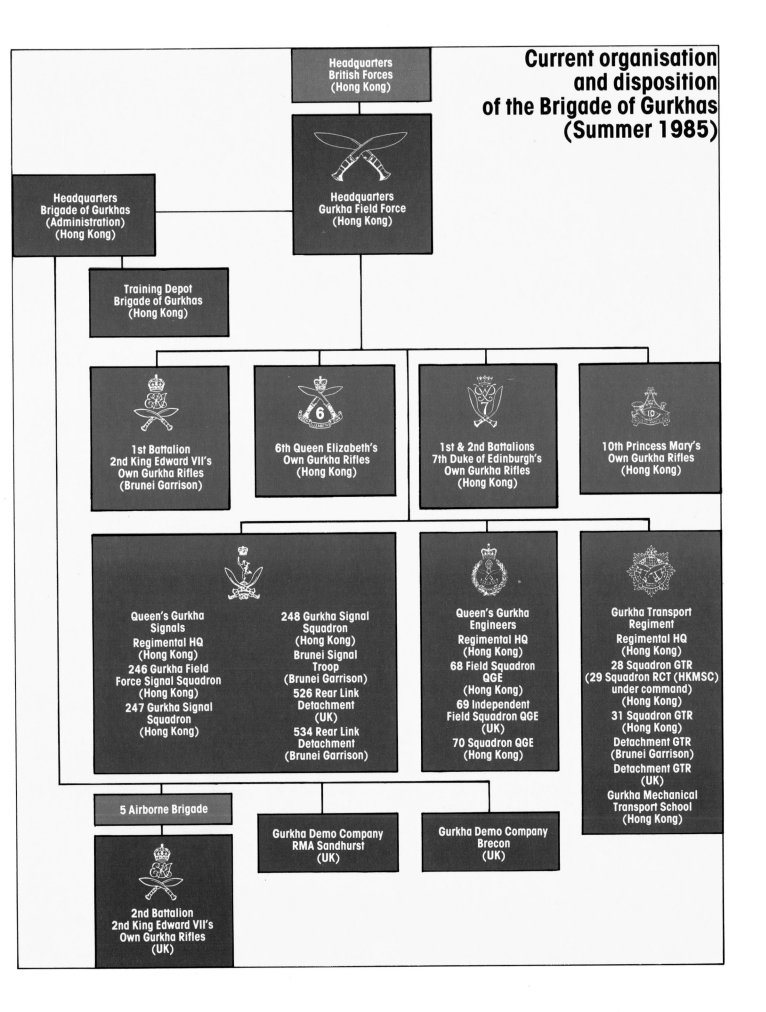

Current organisation and disposition of the Brigade of Gurkhas (Summer 1985)

Headquarters British Forces (Hong Kong)

Headquarters Gurkha Field Force (Hong Kong)

Headquarters Brigade of Gurkhas (Administration) (Hong Kong)

Training Depot Brigade of Gurkhas (Hong Kong)

1st Battalion 2nd King Edward VII's Own Gurkha Rifles (Brunei Garrison)

6th Queen Elizabeth's Own Gurkha Rifles (Hong Kong)

1st & 2nd Battalions 7th Duke of Edinburgh's Own Gurkha Rifles (Hong Kong)

10th Princess Mary's Own Gurkha Rifles (Hong Kong)

Queen's Gurkha Signals
Regimental HQ (Hong Kong)
246 Gurkha Field Force Signal Squadron (Hong Kong)
247 Gurkha Signal Squadron (Hong Kong)

248 Gurkha Signal Squadron (Hong Kong)
Brunei Signal Troop (Brunei Garrison)
526 Rear Link Detachment (UK)
534 Rear Link Detachment (Brunei Garrison)

Queen's Gurkha Engineers
Regimental HQ (Hong Kong)
68 Field Squadron QGE (Hong Kong)
69 Independent Field Squadron QGE (UK)
70 Squadron QGE (Hong Kong)

Gurkha Transport Regiment
Regimental HQ (Hong Kong)
28 Squadron GTR (29 Squadron RCT (HKMSC) under command) (Hong Kong)
31 Squadron GTR (Hong Kong)
Detachment GTR (Brunei Garrison)
Detachment GTR (UK)
Gurkha Mechanical Transport School (Hong Kong)

5 Airborne Brigade

Gurkha Demo Company RMA Sandhurst (UK)

Gurkha Demo Company Brecon (UK)

2nd Battalion 2nd King Edward VII's Own Gurkha Rifles (UK)

ated on the right by 7th Platoon – and they were off. . . . The leading platoons set off like a pack of hounds baying for blood, shouting and shrieking as if they were charging against the final objective . . . It was to be the first but by no means the last time that I was to thank the Almighty for putting me on the same side as the Gurkhas. . . .”

They cleared the village with Tommy-gun and Kukri and when dawn came there were many Germans without heads in the village.

The war over, there were various peace-keeping duties for the Gurkhas to perform including policing Vietnam after the Japanese surrender until the French returned. Five battalions of Gurkhas served in the 20th Indian Division which, commanded by Major-General Douglas Gracey, had been in the thick of the fighting against the Japanese in Burma. But when they arrived in Vietnam they found the Japanese had been allowed to keep their weapons in order to maintain order, and,

Right: World War Two – Gurkha snipers in a shell-torn house in Jubatti. Below: Gurkhas quickly and expertly digging themselves into a burnt-out patch of jungle in Burma, using their Kukris to sharpen the stakes for revettment.

eventually, the former enemies fought alongside one another against the Vietnamese nationalists.

As the historian of the 4th Battalion of the 2nd Goorkhas put it: "Colonel Kitson and his men arrived to be confronted with a paradoxical situation in which former friends and associates were enemies, in which former enemies were auxiliaries, and in which a new war was in the making."

Postwar actions

The great surge of nationalist feeling at the end of the war found the Gurkhas embroiled not only in Vietnam but also in Palestine and the Dutch East Indies. Nationalism was also to bring about great changes in the association between them and the British, for with the partition of India the ten Gurkha regiments in the old Indian Army were divided between the new Indian Army and the British Army. Under a tripartite agreement between Nepal, India and Britain four regiments became an integral part of the British Army. These regiments were: 2nd King Edward VII's Own Goorkha Rifles (The Sirmoor Rifles); 6th Gurkha Rifles (now Queen Elizabeth's Own); 7th Gurkha Rifles (now Duke of Edinburgh's Own) and 10th Gurkha Rifles (now Princess Mary's Own).

It is these regiments along with The Queen's Gurkha Engineers, The Queen's Gurkha Signals and the Gurkha Transport Regiment which make up today's Brigade of Gurkhas.

Both the Indian Gorkhas (they reverted to the old spelling) and the British Gurkhas have fought their battles since then, the Indian regiments notably against the Chinese in 1962, and the British regiments in Malaya, where the 6th Gurkha Rifles served throughout the whole twelve years of the Emergency, and then in Brunei and Borneo.

"VC Saheb" retires

It was in Borneo during the "Confrontation" with Indonesia that Lance Corporal Rambahadur Limbu of the 10th Princess Mary's Own Gurkha Rifles won the last of the Gurkha's VCs. On 21st November 1965 he was part of an advance party when they came across 30 Indonesians entrenched on top of a sheer hill in the jungle. The only approach to the enemy was along a knife-edge ridge and with two other men he crept along it until they were only ten yards from a machine gun post. Then they were spotted. The machine-gunner opened fire, and the Gurkhas were swept by heavy automatic fire from other well-established positions. Both his men were seriously wounded. He reported the situation, then made three attempts to rescue them in full view of the enemy who concentrated their fire on him. Eventually he was able to carry them both back to safety and miraculously emerged unscathed through the hail of fire.

The final paragraph of his official citation reads; "He displayed heroism, self sacrifice and a devotion to duty

Above: Captain Rambahadur Limbu, VC, is seen off by men of the 2nd Battalion, 2nd King Edward VIIth Gurkha Rifles at Church Crookham, Surrey, on his retirement from service.

to his men of the very highest order. His actions on this day reached a zenith of determined, pre-meditated valour which must count amongst the most notable on record and is deserving of the greatest admiration and the highest praise."

Known throughout the Gurkhas as "VC Saheb", he retired after 28 years service on March 25th this year as Captain (Queen's Gurkha Officer) Rambahadur Limbu, VC, MVO. He was seen off in style from Church Crookham and, as befits a man who had served at Buckingham Palace as one of the Queen's Gurkha Orderly Officers he sent a message to the Queen: "It is with sadness that I leave your service after 28 years. On my

Above: Gurkha poses with local Chinese inhabitants in the New Territories during garrison duties in Hong Kong, their first role as soldiers in the British Army.

departure today, I send my most loyal greetings."

The Queen replied: "I too am sad that you are leaving the Gurkhas. I send you my thanks for your years of gallant and distinguished service, and my good wishes for the future."

These messages between the VC Saheb and his Queen symbolise the relationship which was forged between honourable opponents on the field of battle 170 years ago.

Thousands eager to join

There is, however, no shortage of men who would behave as the VC Saheb did. The army needs 400 recruits a year for the Gurkhas, and every year there are 8,000 young men eager to join. Old soldiers are sent out into the hills to do the preliminary selection and when they arrive at villages they are splendidly entertained for they are men of power and influence. But they are firm and between them they send down about 800 potential recruits to the depots at Dharan and Pokhra for medicals and selection. They are already tough for most of them are subsistence farmers scratching out a living at around 7,000 feet. They have few roads and spend their

time scrambling up and down the mountain side, trekking barefoot carrying huge loads – it is sometimes four hours march from the nearest firewood, and fresh water has to be carried in tins up the steep hillsides. Consequently the Gurkhas all have immensely powerful legs but they are prone to tuberculosis and one of the first tests they have to pass is a chest X-ray.

One of the curious results of the Gurkhas' mountain life is that as they never walk on the flat they never learn how to run properly and actually have to be taught how to do so when they start their training. With their huge leg muscles they look terribly ungainly but they soon learn and take to football with enthusiasm.

Two other physical attributes acquired from living in the mountains are excellent eyesight and hearing, unspoiled by the population and noise of the cities. The Gurkhas therefore make excellent shots and scouts.

Although to British eyes they may all look alike, they belong to a tribal or clan system which has different dialects and differing physical traits. The 7th and 10th draw their recruits from Central East Nepal which is inhabited by small, quick-witted Rais and the taller, slower-speaking Limbus; while the 2nd and the 6th look to the Central West where the Gurungs and the Magars live. It is said that the difference between them is that the Gurungs have finer features.

They are all Hindu and while they are fairly relaxed

Above: Gurkhas training in England with the Carl Gustav anti-tank weapon system. Despite suggestions of their outdatedness, Gurkhas take to the new technologies with gusto. Right: Hopeful Gurkha recruit with British officers, circa 1950.

about their religion, no Gurkha will eat cow, although the Gurungs will eat buffalo. Being Hindu a caste system operates but as nearly all the recruits belong to the peasant caste – strangely enough, not the warrior caste – it does not pose too many problems. Like the Arabs and for the same reason the Gurkhas use their right hands for eating and drinking and consider it impolite to hand something to another person with the left hand.

Selection and training

Those that are eventually accepted are flown to Hong Kong for training at the Brigade's main base. This base houses the non-operational Headquarters of the Brigade of Gurkhas, the operational HQ of the Gurkha Field Force which also includes British and locally recruited Chinese, and the training depot for recruits and courses for junior N.C.Os.

The culture shock of arriving at Kai Tak airport is shattering for these young men just down from the solitude of the high hills. To be whisked through the air and land in the centre of Hong Kong's skyscrapers and horn-blowing traffic is like being transported from the

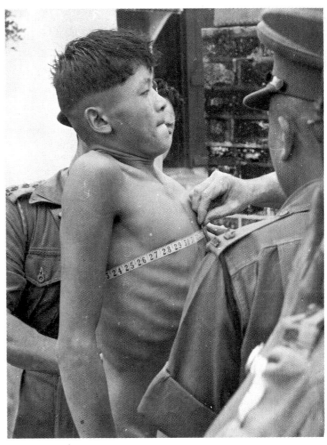

Middle Ages to the Twentieth Century in one day. They have to be taught how to use a western toilet and instructed in the use and dangers of electricity. Nepal is being drawn into the modern world but it has scarcely reached the far hills where most of these young men live.

Their training at Sek Kong in the New Territories lasts ten months and the difference between the bemused peasant boy who passes through the training camp's gates and the immensely smart, self-confident soldier who leaves to join his regiment is astonishing. In that time he has been taught to speak basic English, how to live in the outside world and how to be a soldier of the Queen. There is never any need to teach him to fight. That comes naturally.

Their training is tough and maintains a discipline of the kind now out of fashion with British regiments. For the first three months of their training they are not allowed to smoke or drink and are confined to barracks.

Gurkhas based in Hong Kong train in the New Territories, and also provide a garrison. Left: Jungle training – note the use of non-standard equipment, in this case American M16 Armalite assault rifles. Below, a motor boat patrol, with elementary camouflage, in the New Territories. Gurkhas, though, are notoriously poor sailors.

They spit and polish furiously and as at Church Crookham their accommodation would not be looked upon with favour by other regiments.

Critics complain that their training is dehumanising and that it takes months to rebuild their initiative. But the Gurkhas themselves lap it up and would consider it an insult if the training was softened. Much time is spent on teaching the recruits basic English which is now officially the working language – especially in signals where Gurkhali is not used principally because it would pinpoint the Gurkha positions for any enemy listening in.

From Kukri to Wombat

They are turned into proficient soldiers, the equivalent of any other infantry regiment, and they insist they can do the same job as any other regiment. They are particularly touchy about this because they have so far not been included in BAOR's order of battle on the grounds that they have not been properly trained to take part in armoured warfare. They are, however, trained in all the modern infantry weapons, including the Milan and Wombat anti-tank weapons. As part of the 5th Airborne Brigade the 10th Gurkhas played an "enemy" role in Germany in last year's Operation Lionheart and their

officers insist that they proved their ability to operate in the "armoured environment."

Curiously, the only infantry weapon in which they are not given any fighting training is the kukri. They are taught how to perform ceremonial drill with it, but when it comes to lopping off heads they are expected to be able to do that without being taught.

On being accepted into one of the regiments the Gurkha will either be kept in Hong Kong for training and internal security duties – these days mainly picking up fugitives from Communist China – or posted to the battalion serving in Brunei at the request – and expense – of the Sultan of Brunei, or will come to Church Crookham. The battalions have a system of rotation for these postings. Each battalion serves two years in the United Kingdom followed by four years in Hong Kong, two in Brunei and then back to Hong Kong for a further two years before starting the sequence again.

There are other postings: to the Jungle School in Brunei, to the Demonstration Company at Sandhurst or the Demonstration Company at the NCO Training Wing

Below: Gurkhas training in the Malaysian jungle in January 1985, playing cards and preparing a simple meal of meat and rice. Mountain men by birth, they nonetheless adapt.

Above: Gurkha officer giving salute during a parade in the UK. Older officers are usually recruited from the ranks, although a new breed of Sandhurst trained officer is beginning to appear in the Brigade. Officers thus schooled will be in a position to attain high ranks.

at Brecon and four-month long postings to Korea where a large platoon of Gurkhas forms part of the United Nations Honour Guard. There are also something like a thousand Gurkha soldiers in Nepal at any one time, either working at the Dharan base or travelling to and from their homes on leave.

Long trek home on leave

This, despite the opening up of the country by road and air is still a long process for many. The soldier going on leave is flown from Hong Kong to Katmandu but if he does not live in one of the districts served by the buses which labour up the precipitous mountain roads he must walk home just like his forefathers and this can take up to ten days.

He gets Nepal leave of six months after serving for three years and after his second leave at the end of six years service he can marry, or, if he is already married, can apply for his family to join him in Hong Kong. But

married quarters are scarce and many men are disappointed at first try.

The culture shock for the wives when they arrive is even greater than for the soldiers. To be carried on a magic carpet from a hut with no water and an existence which revolves round maize, rice, salt and goatmeat and very basic clothing to the glitter and high fashion of the Hong Kong shops brings about a fundamental change in outlook which has to be carefully handled by the Gurkhas' welfare service.

In the long run it means an even more fundamental change for the children. They go to the Gurkha school, learn rudimentary English and take part in all those activities pursued in a normal English school and when they return to Nepal they take with them attitudes and a knowledge of the world quite apart from those of children brought up in Nepal.

Many of them follow their fathers and join his regiment, but they have to go back to Nepal to do so in order that no favouritism is shown. However, the "line-boys" have the obvious advantage of being able to speak some English and being steeped in Regimental lore.

Officers and gentlemen

The prospects for bright recruits are good. They can become Queen's Gurkha Officers (QGOs) who rank somewhere between warrant officers and full commissions. They are usually old hands who have worked their way up through the ranks and serve either as platoon commanders or as deputy commanders of companies. But another type of officer has made his appearance under a scheme started in the 1950s. He is the Sandhurst Commissioned Gurkha who has been to the Royal Military Academy just like regular British officers. It is among these officers that the advantage of having been a "line-boy" and attending the Gurkha High School in Hong Kong becomes evident. One of these new-style officers has now been to Staff College and is a Lieutenant Colonel.

But even a man who remains a Rifleman for the whole of his career returns to Nepal a rich and respected man, able to buy himself a house and land. The Gurkha really needs no encouragement to save money. That, after all is one of the main reasons he joined up besides the special honour of serving with the Regiment.

He is happier than most soldiers to stay in barracks, drinking rum – nearest thing to his native brew – and lager in the NAAFI or watching Hindustani films at the camp cinema. There is also a piped radio system which relays programmes in Gurkhali prepared in Hong Kong. His British officers also make sure he does not overspend. Gambling, of which he is fond, is only allowed on the religious festival of Diwali and even then only a certain amount may be won or lost. The reason for this, according to Gurkha folklore, is that one man once gambled his wife and lost and she, shamed, killed herself. Apocryphal or not, the British officers are determined to protect their men from the evils of the world.

Above: One of the new breed Sandhurst cadet officers is cheered by his countrymen. Right: Field Marshal Lord Roberts, VC, in a painting at the Gurkha Museum at Church Crookham. One of the 'father figures', he won his VC during the Indian Mutiny.

British officers learn Gurkha ways

This paternalism has always been one of the features of Gurkha regiments. When a young British officer joins a regiment one of the first things he does is to attend a two-month Nepalese Language Qualification Course at the Hong Kong training depot and he is expected to immerse himself in Gurkha culture and tradition. He is told, for example, never to shout at a Gurkha because this would only lower his prestige in the Gurkha's eyes. The 2nd Goorkhas are proud of what they call "The Sirmoor System" which, developed from a Rifle regiment's tradition of independent action, emphasises the responsibility of every officer to maintain his own standards and thus develop a mutual relationship of trust with his men.

The point is that if a Gurkha loses faith in an officer that officer is finished, but once trust is established the Gurkha will follow him to hell and back.

There are only 17 British officers to a Gurkha batta-

R KHARD SCOLLINS 1985

lion and while they may be seconded to other units to improve their military skills – the SAS is a favourite – the very nature of Gurkha work puts them outside the main stream of promotion. This means that most of the young men who join either want a bit of adventure in the Far East or belong to a "Gurkha family" and would never dream of serving in another regiment.

It is the family tradition of service both among the Gurkhas and their British officers which give the regiments their very special cohesion. The Gurkhas have also been fortunate in the number of distinguished officers on whom they have looked as father figures: Their founder, General Young; Field Marshal Lord Roberts who won his VC during the Mutiny and died at the age of 82 while visiting his beloved Gurkhas in France in November 1914; Field Marshal Lord Slim, a former Gurkha officer who always turned to them when the going got rough in Burma; Lieutenant General Sir Francis Tuker who wrote their story in "Gorkha: The Story of the Gurkhas of Nepal"; General Sir Walter Walker of one of India's great military families; Brigadier "Mad Mike" Calvert who commanded Gurkhas during the Chindit operations in Burma and Field Marshal Sir Edwin Bramall former Chief of the Defence Staff and presently the Colonel of the 2nd Goorkhas.

Regiment looks after its own

These are only a few of the senior officers who have played a major role in Gurkha history. They are roles which go beyond soldiering. There is not another regiment with the "aftercare" that the Gurkhas lavish on their former soldiers. Some 16,000 pensions are paid to Gurkhas who have retired since 1948 when they were incorporated in the British Army. Originally these pensions were doled out by officers of the regiments who went round the hills with a sackfull of money and an armed escort – and occasionally suffered the embarrassment of running out of money. Today, young officers are still assigned from Hong Kong to pay the pensions but now the pensioners trek in to a number of specified points at a date arranged the previous year.

The pensions are not all the help the Gurkhas get. In 1967 when cutbacks in the number of battalions threatened to swamp the regimental welfare service, an appeal was launched which eventually raised over a million pounds from men who had fought alongside the Gurkhas.

This money, from all over the world, was invested and the profits are used to help families in distress caused by landslides and floods and to pay pensions to widows, for the government pension ends when the former soldier dies. The Canadians were late coming into this scheme because it took time for the fund to be granted charity status but the delay worked well in the end for once the charity status was agreed, the Cana-

Left: Combat-equipped Gurkha with Sterling submachine gun in tropical DPM fatigues.

dian government paid two dollars into the fund for every dollar raised privately. This money is used to build suspension bridges, schools and to provide running water.

It is, moreover used to the benefit not only of Ex-Gurkhas but for all Nepalese and in so doing helps ease the friction caused for example when welfare funds are used to help a former soldier rebuild his house while his neighbour who has lost his house in the same disaster gets nothing because he has never been a soldier.

Uncle Sam lends a hand

The Gurkha's have another source of income, strangely enough, from the United States. Called the Gurkha Welfare Trust Foundation, it was set up by Mrs Ellice McDonald, an American who fell in love with the Gurkhas when she saw their band perform at a Tattoo in Toronto, Canada.

These various schemes are co-ordinated by the Brigade Welfare Officer at Dharan who has working for him a number of project managers, all of them ex-servicemen.

All then would seem to be well with the Gurkhas; members of an elite, respected men with a long tradition of courage who have won their place in British military history by valour and military prowess; men who can retire and live well, safe in the knowledge that their regiment will come to their aid if they fall on hard times. The truth is that the Gurkhas are currently facing one of the most dangerous times in their history. For now their very existence is threatened.

In 1997, just twelve years away, Hong Kong will be handed back to China. Not only will the Gurkha role there be wiped out but so will the Brigade Headquarters, the Field Force, the Training Depot and the School. Burma Lines, Cassino Lines and Gallipoli Lines, named after Gurkha battle honours, which house three of the battalions now stationed there will be in Chinese hands.

What then, will happen to the Gurkhas? The Sultan of Brunei wants the battalion guarding his country to stay on and the battalion at Church Crookham is valuable because it frees a British battalion for service in Northern Ireland and is an integral part of the Home Defence forces. But that is not enough to justify the resettling of the Hong Kong organisation somewhere else. The cost will be great even though the Gurkhas are "cheap" soldiers, costing the government about a third less than other regiments. So if the Gurkhas are to survive some other role must be found for them.

There are non-Gurkha senior officers who argue that they are an anachronism in modern military terms and would fight their retention if it meant the end of a county regiment which has been fully trained in mechanised warfare. On a value for money basis, they argue, the Gurkha cannot be compared with a man trained in computer-style warfare. Given the present economic climate in which the forces are being asked to cut and cut again, this is a powerful argument.

Above: Gurkha of the Queen's Gurkha Signals using a battlefield communications radio. The Brigade provides its own Regiments of Signals, Transport and Engineers, as well as a separate Airborne Brigade and specialist Demolition Companies.

The Gurkhas who have faced cuts before, being whittled down to their present six battalions plus their support units, know that this is probably the period of greatest danger in the whole of their history and they are mustering all the support they can among the Gurkha "Mafia" which still wields much power in the Ministry of Defence.

Controversy continues over retention of the Regiment

They can mount powerful arguments. The first of these will be the effect the disbandment of the Gurkhas would have in Nepal and Brunei. It would be seen as a betrayal by the Nepalese government and would also lose the country valuable hard currency. In an area where the Russians are playing "The Great Game" with skill and vigour the friendship of Nepal, for so long a faithful ally of the British Crown, cannot be lightly risked.

The Sultan of Brunei has already fought off one attempt to withdraw the battalion serving in his country. Under the Defence Review economics of 1975, the two battalions of the 2nd Goorkhas were to be amalgamated and the battalion in Brunei was to be the one for the chop. The Sultan fought back, kicking up such a fuss that the withdrawal was first postponed until 1983 and then cancelled, leaving the 2nd Goorkhas as the only Gurkha regiment with two battalions. With his oil fields he is, of course, rich enough to afford his own battalion but that would involve delicate diplomatic manouevring with the Nepalese and Indian governments and he would have to rely on free-lance or seconded British officers to run the battalion for him.

With his considerable investments in Britain his voice is likely to be listened to by the government. The loss of the Brunei establishment would also mean the closing down of the Jungle training school and the subsequent loss of all those skills hard-earned in World War Two, Malaysia and Borneo. The re-establishment of the school elsewhere would be both difficult and costly.

The Gurkhas will also call on the lessons of the Falklands in their struggle for survival. They can point out that the struggle not only against Argentines but also against the weather and the terrain proved once again that only the toughest of soldiers can survive in the type of wars the British army is now asked to fight.

It was the Paras and the Marine Commandos who performed best of all in the Falklands and they did so because they were hard, fit, and tuned to fight at close

Below: Platoon photo taken after a Company Exercise in Malaysia in 1985. The weapons include US M16 assault rifles, FN FALs, and the ubiquitous General Purpose Machine Gun.

quarters. These are not computer soldiers and neither are the Gurkhas – everybody at Church Crookham goes on a "ten-mile bash" once a week. They are convinced that the British army still needs them in their traditional role as spearpoint attacking troops, kukri in hand and "Ayozi Gurkhali" on their lips.

At the same time they argue that if they were given the opportunity they could fit happily into BAOR. They consider it a slight that they have not been allotted a place in the order of battle to face the Russians and deny indignantly that the sheer technicality of the modern battle-field has passed them by.

No role in Ulster – but Germany?

They acknowledge that there is one place that they will never be sent: Northern Ireland. The thought of the small brown men prowling the bandit country of South Armagh, kukris ready to lop off a few IRA heads, may give pleasure to many people but it gives the politicians the horrors. But they do insist that they would fit in well with BAOR and their old enemies, the Germans, for whom they have much admiration as soldiers.

The word is that nothing has yet been decided, but as one senior officer put it, "the future of the Gurkhas is being looked at with some trepidation at the highest level."

Perhaps the greatest asset the Gurkhas will have in the forthcoming battle for survival is the enormous esteem and affection in which they are held by the ordinary British soldier who admires not only their bravery and loyalty but also their sense of fun. But even that may not be sufficient to defeat the forces of military economy, perhaps the most powerful and most blind of all military forces.

It would be a sad day that marked the end of the long and honourable association between the Gurkhas and the British, two unmilitary but warlike peoples.

It was Sir Ralph Turner, Professor of Sanskrit and sometime Adjutant of the 2nd Battalion The 3rd Queen Alexandra's Own Gurkha Rifles, who best put this association into words: "My thoughts return to you who were my comrades, the stubborn and indomitable peasants of Nepal. Once more I hear the laughter with which you greeted every hardship. Once more I see you shivering in your bivouacs or about your camp fires, on forced march or in the trenches, now shivering with wet and cold, now scorched by a pitiless and burning sun. Uncomplaining you endure hunger and thirst and wounds; and at the last your unwavering lines disappear into the smoke and wrath of battle. Bravest of the brave, most generous of the generous, never had a country more faithful friends than you."

Right: Gurkha Rifleman poses with the traditional Kukri. They are not trained in the use of these weapons, but grow up with them in the relatively peaceful hills of Nepal where the Kukri is seen more as an all-round domestic tool than a decapitating device.

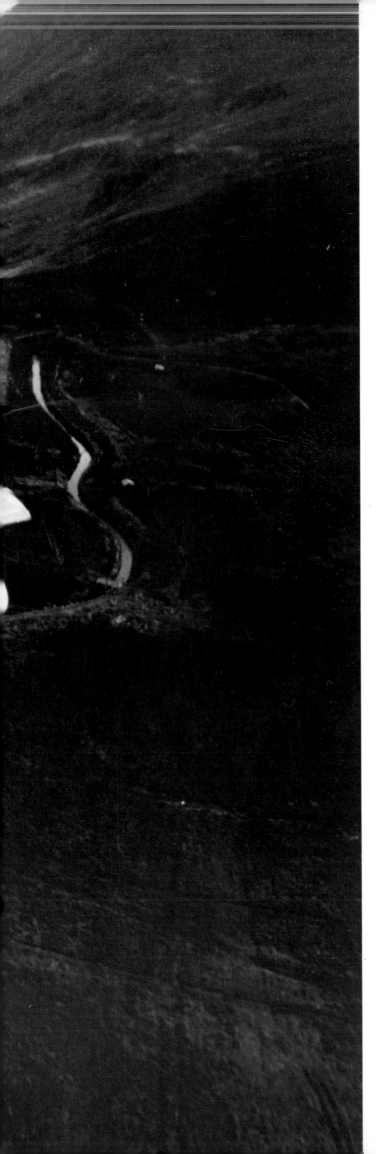

Chapter 5

AIR WAR: RESTRUCTURE AND RE-EQUIP

Not just the RAF, but also the Navy and Army air arms have been involved in changes since the end of the Falklands War. Many of the lessons learnt then have been acted upon, and now some results are beginning to show.

Interdiction-Strike Tornado carrying ECM pods and long range fuel tanks on underwing pylons.

It is now three years since the end of the Falklands War in June 1982, and sufficient time has elapsed for the dust to settle (both literally and metaphorically) and so give objective analysts a real chance to assess the war and its impact on the British armed forces. Not the least of these results has been the Conservative government's implementation of its 'Fortress Falklands' policy, in military terms the inevitable consequence of British determination not to abandon the islands which cost the country so dear in 1982. Opponents of the government's policy can and do argue that the concept of 'Fortress Falklands' costs far more than the islands are worth, but given the intransigence of the Argentine authorities in refusing to end the state of hostilities despite their avowal to proceed henceforth only by diplomatic means, the government's position is militarily inevitable. There can be no denial, however, of the fact that the 'Fortress Falklands' policy is costing the UK much in financial and military terms. Quite apart from the capital outlay and recurrent expenses of the garrison and its forces, the drain on British resources (occasioned by the need to keep substantial quantities of men and large amounts of equipment in the Falklands, to keep them supplied, to replace them at regular intervals, and to build up the infrastructure for a substantial garrison many thousands of miles from home) is having a profound effect on the British defence posture.

Combat experience "profitable offshoot"

This posture is already straitened by the demands of the situation in Northern Ireland and in Belize, already having their effect on forces generally optimized for the type of mobile warfare anticipated in the event of hostilities with the Warsaw Pact. However, it can be argued that a profitable offshoot of the Falklands War was the sheer volume of operational experience garnered by the British forces during the six-week campaign, which for the first time saw the combat deployment of many new weapon systems in a technologically-intensive conflict. Some of the lessons are ones that were relearned (the tendency of equipment to fail under adverse conditions, the expenditure of ammunition at far higher rates than anticipated, the need to place reliance on men rather than machines and, in the air, the overall importance of an effective early warning system), but others are novel, at least in their specific applications if not in their very concept: typical of these are the desirability of inflight-refuelling capability for tactical aircraft such as the BAe Harrier and Sea Harrier family, the absolute need for such a refuelling capability on longer-range

Below: RAF VC10s re-fuelling in flight, operated by No 101 Squadron based at RAF Brize Norton. Nine of these new RAF acquisitions are currently in service, with others to follow.

machines such as the Lockheed Hercules transport and BAe Nimrod maritime reconnaissance aircraft, the advantages of air-to-air missile capability for the self defence of tactical aircraft, the absolute necessity of radar-controlled close-in weapons mountings for the defence of warships against sea-skimming anti-ship missiles and low-flying attack aircraft, the desirability of maintaining a force of at least three 'Invincible' class light aircraft-carriers, and the importance of updating the British air forces' offensive weapons types.

"Smarter" weapons needed

In this last category, it is worth noting, the British relied almost exclusively on free-fall 'iron' bombs and unguided rockets during the Falklands campaign, the limited use of guided weapons resulting from poor performance when such weapons were used. It was clear, however, that such weapons were of very limited effectiveness even in the Falklands, and would be next to useless in the context of a European war against an enemy with advanced and numerous air-defence weapons. Thus one of the most important lessons of the Falklands War was the need to improve aircraft weapon capabilities with more advanced 'smart' weapons (both free-fall and powered types) used in conjuction with more numerous airborne and ground designating systems. This need has been fully appreciated since 1982, and RAF procurement of such weapons has been matched by army purchases of appropriate designating systems. Just as importantly, perhaps, this and the other lessons of the Falklands War has been made available to the UK's partners within the NATO alliance, and the implementation of these lessons have been of incalculable benefit in improving the alliance's military capabilities. And whereas many of the lessons have been small in scale, and thus of significance only en masse, the two most important areas crucial to long-term success on an individual basis: these are the need for far greater stockpiles of basic munitions for all three services, and the need for greatly enhanced air defences against low-flying aircraft and missiles. In this latter category are attacks coming in head-on (and so presenting only a small target that must be engaged successfully with a high volume of fire in the closing stages of the attack) and attackers crossing the target at a high rate (and so presenting the defenders with difficult fire-control and mechanical problems such as lead-computing and adequate traverse speeds).

Air defence dilemma

The UK's air forces are thus placed in a difficult position: clearly the main threat remains that of the Warsaw Pact organization and any westward drive it may launch in Europe, while there remain a number of diversions from this primary (and indeed monumentally difficult) task. No one can doubt that the European role is indeed the main task faced by the Royal Air Force and the Army Air Corps, while the Fleet Air Arm (with RAF support) must help to insure that the sealanes to the North American continent are kept open for the transit of the vast quantities of materiel that would have to shipped over from the US and Canada in time of crisis or war (estimates put this quantity at 100,000 or more tons per day to sustain a NATO effort against a maximum-intensity Warsaw Pact offensive); the FAA must also be able to provide air support for Royal Marine forces, a proportion of which is earmarked for service well away from the NATO Central Front and Atlantic/English Channel primary regions in northern Norway to guard against any Soviet advance from the Murmansk region. And in the context of the European role of the RAF it should be remembered that this means not just support of the British Army of the Rhine by RAF Germany, but also the air defence of the UK, which is earmarked as the alliance's main base for the receipt of supplies and materiel flowing across the Atlantic before further distribution to forces needing them in Europe proper. This defensive task within the UK Air Defence Region is much complicated by the need to support detachments in other parts of the world: notable amongst these are the Falklands, the staging post of Ascension Island en route to the Falklands, Belize in Central America, Cyprus with its two Sovereign Base Areas (helping also to cover any Soviet advance towards the eastern and central Mediterranean regions), Gibraltar and Hong Kong.

Falklands expenditure

Apart from that in West Germany, the largest overseas RAF presence is in the Falklands, which apart from absorbing significant quantities of manpower and materiel have also swallowed vast sums from the exchequer. Costs are notoriously difficult to quantify, but it is reckoned that in the four years up to March 1988 the Falklands will have used some £3,790 million which would have been more usefully deployed elsewhere: of this total £3,000 million are directly attributable to the Argentine invasion, the British recapture of the islands and reconstruction/re-equipment costs up to March 1986; £490 million are earmarked for 1987 expenditure in the islands' defence; and a further £300 million are allocated to 1988. This is a prodigious sum by any standards, and in greater detail the breakdown includes £780 million for the recapture of the Falklands, £1,210 for the replacement of equipment lost in battle or otherwise destroyed in the campaign, and £550 million for the construction of a new military infrastructure for the islands. Yearly running costs are expected to be in the order of £180 million for a garrison of about 4,000 declining to 2,000-3,000 once the new airport/air base at Mount Pleasant is fully operational. Another cost factor to be taken into account is that of replacement for the equipment that in the Falklands has a considerably lower life expectancy than would have otherwise been the case. All in all, therefore, there can be no denial of the fact that the need to defend the Falklands against the

threat of renewed Argentine aggression is extremely high. There are, of course, political and moral reasons for this British stance, and it should be added that there may well also be economic reasons if the sea and/or sea bed prove fruitful. And should one object that a British military presence of the current magnitude is not needed in the light of Argentina's current pursuit of sovereignty by non-military means, it need be borne in mind that current non-military means can easily be replaced overnight by overt military action in a nation as unstable as Argentina, which has a history of civilian rule falling to military juntas.

New airport opened at Mount Pleasant by Prince Andrew

The Falkland Islands lie some 8,000 miles from the UK, but a mere 400 miles from mainland Argentina. As the islands possessed before the Argentine invasion only one airfield with a paved runway (Port Stanley, with a runway measuring only 4,200 ft), air communications with the mother country were impossible. Instead air communications with the Falklands had to be routed through Argentina, a service to the islands being maintained with Fokker F.27 Friendship twin-turboprop transports. Such a link was clearly undesirable (indeed impossible) after the Falklands War, and an initial priority was to extend the runway at Port Stanley so that it could receive Lockheed Hercules C.1 four-turboprop transports providing the 'air bridge' link to the islands

Above: The First TriStar passenger transport to land at the new Mount Pleasant airport, May 1985. The trip takes 19 hours with a stop-over at Ascension Island.

from the staging point at Wideawake Airfield on Ascension Island, midway between the UK and the Falklands. AM2 aluminium alloy matting was used to extend the runway to 6,000 ft, but the Hercules link was clearly not the answer to the air communications problem: the link could be severed by adverse weather over the Falklands, the Hercules has only a modest load, and the trip took a gruelling 13 hours in the air with the aid of at least one inflight-refuelling by BAe Victor K.2 tankers later supplemented by Hercules C.1K conversions. Moreover, the cost of each return trip to the Falklands (including the out-and-return legs by BAe VC10 C.1 transport linking Ascension Island with the UK) was £155,000. It was decided, therefore, that though the capital cost would be high, a new airport-cum-air base should be built in the Falklands as Port Stanley could not be extended farther for geographical reasons. The choice fell on a site near Fitzroy on East Falkland, and here RAF Mount Pleasant has been built at a cost estimated at £276 million (including a new garrison HQ). A further £128 million are allocated to a new port and some 30 miles of road linking Mount Pleasant and the nearby port with Port Stanley.

Mount Pleasant was opened on 12 May 1985 by HRH The Prince Andrew, though the first landing by one of

Above: Phantom of 42 Squadron, based in Germany. The new airport will make the rapid deployment of fighter aircraft from Europe quicker and more efficient in the event of renewed threat.

No.216 Squadron's nine Lockheed TriStar C.1s from RAF Brize Norton was made on 1 May 1985. Though No.216 Squadron will make three round flights per week with the wide-body TriStar from November 1985, the service will be flown between June and November by Boeing 747s of British Airways.

One runway operational

Though only the first of two runways is currently operational (an east-west runway measuring 8,000 ft), this already allows a wide-body transport to fly in reinforcements for the garrison (a TriStar can carry 240 fully-equipped men) with greater facility than possible via the Hercules 'air bridge': a TriStar from Brize Norton can arrive in the Falklands after a 19-hour trip (including a 90-minute halt at Ascension), and deliver its troops in far fresher condition. Just as important in these parsimonious days, the price of a round trip is much reduced in seat/mile terms, and the inauguration of the full service to Mount Pleasant will save the RAF £25 million per year in fuel and other associated costs. Hercules services to Port Stanley are being reduced from five to two per week, flying freight only, and the opening of Mount Pleasant's secondary north-south 5,000-ft runway in February 1986 will permit Port Stanley to revert

to civil traffic. Port Stanley will retain facilities (arrester gear etc) for emergency use of the airfield by the defence forces on the islands.

Though the UK's ability to reinforce the garrison substantially and with minimum delay will make possible a considerable reduction in the garrison strength on the islands, the fact that Argentina neither declared war in the first place nor admitted an end to hostilities means that substantial forces have to be maintained as a deterrent. Even after the end of hostilities proper, the Argentine air force continued to make probing flights with high-performance Dassault-Breguet Mirage III fighters to test the RAF's air-defence capability and to keep the garrison forces on edge. Though this practice ceased with the inception of President Alfonsin's civil government in Argentina, the RAF maintains useful long-range air-defence forces in the islands. Apart from the fact that they are needed aboard their parent carriers, the FAA's Sea Harriers would not be suitable for the current air-defence needs of the Falklands by reason of their comparative lack of range and short-range missile armament (AIM-9L Sidewinder). Though this latter aspect is being remedied in the Sea Harrier FRS.2 version under development with Ferranti Blue Vixen pulse-Doppler (look-down) radar matched to medium-range AIM-120 AMRAAM radar-guided fire-and-forget missiles, the air defence of the Falklands now rests with the McDonnell Douglas Phantom FGR.1s of No.23 Squadron, which replaced the Phan-

Det of No. 29 Squadron in April 1983. The Phantoms carry a primary armament of AIM-7E Sparrow or Skyflash medium-range semi-active radar-homing air-to-air missiles.

The air-defence force for the Falklands operates in conjunction with a Ferranti Air Defence Ground Environment Mk 4 system, which integrates the data provided by two Plessey AR3D 270-mile-range 3-D radars, TPS-63 radars captured from the Argentines, and an assortment of lesser radars on the two main islands of the group. This highly effective system is more than a match for anything the Argentine air forces can presently throw at the Falklands, and is primarily responsible for the patrols operated by the Phantoms out to the limits of the Protection Zone, and also provides target information as and when required for the Rapier surface-to-air missile units deployed at Port Stanley, Mount Pleasant and San Carlos.

Land-based Harriers limited in Falklands

During the Falklands War the Harrier GR.3s of the RAF played only a small part, being particularly hampered by their lack of range, and by the limited targets available after they were able to come ashore. However, it was realized that land-based Harriers together with adequ-

Above: Skyflash medium-range air-to-air missile being fired from an ADV Tornado. The semi-active radar homing missile also equips the GR1 Phantoms of 23 Squadron currently in the Falklands.

ate numbers of 'smart' weapons and appropriate designators would be a powerful deterrent against renewed Argentine landing, and to this end a HarDet (Harrier Detachment) was provided in the islands for the close support of army forces. Still carrying the Sidewinder AAMs with which they were fitted during the journey south for Operation 'Corporate', the Harrier force has been designated No. 1453 Flight since August 1983 and now flies five aircraft. As with the Harrier squadrons in RAF Germany, No. 1453 Flight frequently practises dispersed deployment to mitigate the threat of runway destruction by 'dibber' bombs. Apart from RAF Stanley, the airstrip at Goose Green receives frequent detachments, and use is also made of other landing sites in the islands.

Other combat aircraft are not based in the islands, but detachments have been made for trials purposes: in October 1983 a Nimrod MR. 2 maritime reconnaissance and anti'-submarine aircraft visited Port Stanley, and a few months earlier (March 1983) a pair of BAe Buccaneer S.2Bs landed at Stanley. It is clear, therefore, that powerful reinforcements for land and maritime operations could quickly be despatched to bolster 'Fortress Falklands' as required.

Increased operational radius is provided to these combat assets by the availability in the Falklands at present of No.1312 Flight, which is based at RAF Stanley with Hercules C.1K tanker aircraft, though the primary responsibility of these interim tankers is the inflight-refuelling of probe-fitted Hercules C.1P and Hercules C.3P transporters operating the current 'air bridge' from Ascension Island.

Helicopters vital in rugged terrain

Another facet of air operations whose importance was emphasized by the Falklands War was the value of helicopter transport in terrain as unfavourable to wheeled and tracked transport as the Falklands. The RAF provides a heavy-lift capability with No.1310 Flight (previously ChinDet) based at Kelly's Garden with an average strength of four Boeing Vertol Chinook HC.1 twin-rotor helicopters, and the detachment of Westland Sea King HAR.3s provided from No.202 Squadron is now styled No.1564 Flight and also based at Kelly's Garden. As its primary search-and-rescue role is not often in demand, No.1564 Flight operates in the utility role with the aid of three Sikorsky S-61Ns chartered from Bristow Helicopters. Rotary-wing air strength is also pro-

Right: A Chinook heavy-lift helicopter of RAF Gutersloh in Germany with under-slung loads. Below: Early flight of Lynx-3 helicopter, seen armed with Hellfire anti-tank missiles and canon, during US army trials. It is to equip the Royal Navy.

vided by the Royal Navy, whose warships embark Westland Lynx HAS.2/3, Westland Wasp HAS.1 and Sea King HAS.5 helicopters according to individual ships' roles and sizes. Army air strength is based at Lookout Camp in the form of the Falklands Garrison Air Squadron. This is a composite unit equipped with Lynx AH.1s, Aerospatiale Gazelle AH.1s and Westland Scout AH.1s, and provides a useful tactical reconnaissance and light aircraft capability, though maintenance problems have been encountered with the Lynxes, and the Gazelle proved considerably less than perfect during the Falklands War.

Though all is currently peaceful in the Falklands, the air forces of the garrison are kept at a high state of readiness, and every opportunity is taken to fly exercises in the almost unpopulated regions of these remote islands. It is likely that the Harriers will soon return to the UK, for trials have confirmed that the type can fly out directly to the islands with the aid of tanker aircraft, and keeping in so distant an area an aircraft type optimized for the European arena is at best problematical.

While the squadrons and flights operating in the Falklands generally make do with current equipment, there appears to be little likelihood that combat aircraft of the very latest generation will find their way to the Falklands garrison, for the Argentine threat does not warrant such a deployment over the needs of the threat posed by the Warsaw Pact. So while the new generation of strike, interception, close support and airborne early warning aircraft may be seen in the Falklands on detachment, these primary air assets are generally reserved for the high-threat scenario in Europe, leaving the Falklands to soldier on with aircraft that are approaching obsolescence but still more than a match for the Argentine front-line inventory.

RAF 'facelift' to be implemented

The RAF has indeed just entered a decade of crucial importance in its history, for some £14,000 million is currently earmarked for the widespread production of new aircraft for the service, which is faced by mass obsolescence of its present aircraft at a time when the quantitative and qualitative strength of the potential foe has never been higher. The cornerstones of this re-equipment programme are the Panavia Tornado (in Tornado GR.1 strike and Tornado F.2 interceptor versions); the BAe Nimrod AEW.3 airborne warning and control platform; the McDonnell Douglas/BAe Harrier GR.5 close-support aircraft modelled on the Harrier II developed by McDonnell Douglas for the US Marine Corps; the revitalized transport/tanker force made up of Lockheed TriStar C.1s and BAe VC10 K.2/3s supplemented by stretched Lockheed Hercules C.3s for tactical transport; and the Embraer/Shorts Tucano trainer. And in the slightly longer term the RAF is seeking a replacement for the Sepecat Jaguar strike and reconnaissance aircraft, the McDonnell Douglas Phantom interceptor, and the Westland Wessex and Aerospatiale

Above Left: Hawk in aggressive role carrying anti-shipping missile on the centreline, and Sidewinder air-to-air missiles on the wing pylons. Below left: Early flight of the GR5 Harrier 2 VSTOL aircraft. Above: Tornado ADV (Air Defence Variant) armed with 4 Skyflash under the fuselage, 2 Sidewinders and drop tanks.

tactical transport helicopters. It is hoped that these two new types will begin to enter service in the mid-1990s to complement the aircraft of the current new generation, which will be approaching the mid point of their careers as front-line aircraft.

Operational air assets in the UK fall under the control of RAF Strike Command, which has three operational groups: No.1 Group is tasked with strike and tactical support, No.11 Group is entrusted with the air defence of the UK Air Defence Region, and No.38 Group is responsible for maritime matters. Also part of Strike Command is the RAF's transport force.

No.1 Group is the main UK operator of the superlative Tornado GR.1 strike aircraft, which is now on the strength of the British component of the Trinational Tornado Training Establishment at RAF Cottesmore, the Tornado Weapons Conversion Unit (shadowed as No.45 Squadron) and No.9 Squadron at RAF Honington, and Nos 27 and 617 Squadrons at RAF Marham. Though some of the aircraft operated by the TTTE are designated Tornado GR.1T to reflect the fact that they have dual controls, the Tornado aircraft in service with the RAF are magnificent blind first-pass interdictor/

strike aircraft, without doubt unexcelled in their designed role anywhere in the world. There has been some carping criticism of the type in US politico-military circles (on the grounds of its weight and electronics), but this criticism recieved the ultimate rebuff when RAF Tornadoes walked away with some of the US Air Force's premier prizes during 1984 combat competitions in the US.

Fitted with a Texas Instruments ground-mapping and terrain-following radar, an inertial navigation system, Doppler navigation, an advanced head-up display, a Marconi modular radar-warning receiver and an ARI.23246 Sky Shadow modular jammer pod, the Tornado GR.1 has excellent radius of action thanks to its substantial internal and external fuel capacities, can operate over long distances at supersonic speeds at altitudes as low as 200 ft without undue airframe or crew fatigue as a result of the variable-geometry layout and advanced avionics/fly-by-wire flight system, and can deliver an enormous range of offensive weapons with pinpoint accuracy in a first pass in any weather conditions by day or night. The nominal weapon load is 18,000 lb, and 'smart' weapons are guided by a Ferranti laser ranger and marked-target seeker, which may be supplemented by the Westinghouse 'Pave Spike' equip-

Left: The future of Britain's air defence combines Nimrod AEW with Tornado interceptor. Below: Embraer/Shorts Tucano which beat stiff opposition to become the future RAF basic trainer. Above right: Jaguars of 20 Sqn, RAF Germany. Below right: RAF Harrier GR3s break formation during low-level exercise.

Above: Navigator/Weapons Officer back seat position of Interdictor-Strike Tornado with combined radar and map display flanked by tabular TV screens.

ment. The avionics of the Tornado GR.1 will certainly be augmented and updated, and new weapons envisaged for this remarkable aircraft (also in service with the Aviazione Militare Italiana and with the West German Luftwaffe and Marineflieger) include the ALARM anti-radiation missile.

From airliner to air-tanker – the fleet expands

Inflight-refuelling support for these and other tactical aircraft is provided by the RAF's tanker fleet. Long based on the venerable Handley Page Victor K.2 (22 of which are in service with Nos 55 and 57 Squadrons and with No.232 Operational Conversion Unit, all at RAF Marham), this tanker force was revealed as wholly inadequate by the demands of the Falklands War, whose tanker demands made serious inroads into the airframe lives left to the Victors. The emergency conversion of six Avro Vulcans to K.2 tanker configuration ameliorated the short-term situation, but it was clear that definitive steps had to be taken. Work had already started on the conversion of four VC10 and five Super VC10 airliners into VC10 K.2 and VC10 K.3 tankers (with another 12 airframes available for later conversion), but it was decided to bolster this capability by the purchase

of nine TriStar 500s for conversion into dual-role tanker/strategic transport aircraft. The VC10s now serve with No.101 Squadron at RAF Brize Norton, while the TriStar operator is No.216 Squadron, also at Brize Norton.

To complement its 220 Tornado GR.1 strike aircraft, the RAF also has on order 165 examples of the Tornado F.2 long-range interceptor variant for service with squadrons No. 11 Group in the defence of the UK Air Defence Region. Based closely on the GR.1, the Tornado F.2 has a lengthened fuselage for additional fuel and the semi-recessed carriage of four Skyflash, Sparrow or AIM-120 air-to-air missiles, and a revised avionics suite. The lengthened fuselage has the additional advantage of improving the type's aerodynamics, with useful increments in supersonic acceleration and reductions in supersonic drag. This all adds up to a very useful interceptor that has displayed an ability to fly a combat air patrol of 2.33 hours at a radius of 374 miles from base while armed with four Skyflash and two Sidewinder air-to-air missiles plus two drop tanks. But this is only part of the whole package, for a major key to the Tornado F.2's remarkable capabilities is the avionics package, centred on the Ferranti Foxhunter nose radar: this is a pulse-Doppler interception set with advanced features that allow it to track between 12 and 20 possible targets while continuing to scan out to a range of 120 or more miles depending on the target's radar cross-section; and

Above: The first two production Tornado F2s en route for delivery to RAF Conningsby Operational Conversion Unit prior to full operational deployment of the type.

as it is a pulse-Doppler equipment, the Foxhunter has look-down capability, which in conjunction with snapdown Skyflash missiles gives the Tornado F.2 a beyond-visual-range look-down/shoot-down capability. And for close-range engagements the Tornado F.2 can also carry Sidewinder IR-homing missiles, with an inbuilt Mauser 27-mm cannon (also carried by the Tornado GR.1) for dogfighting engagements. The Tornado F.2 carries very advanced electronic countercountermeasures, has provision for an electro-optical visual augmentation system for the verification of radar targets beyond unaided optical range (though this EO VAS has yet to be fitted), and is fitted with secure datalink equipment to operate in conjuction with AWACS-type aircraft.

Obsolescent interceptors on way out

The first two Tornado F.2 aircraft were delivered as a basis for No.229 Operational Conversion Unit at RAF Coningsby during November 1984, and the first operational squadrons will begin to form on the type at the beginning of 1986, probably at RAF Leeming. This will finally permit the retirement or relegation of some of the RAF's obsolescent interceptor force.

The Tornado F.2 is fully capable of autonomous operation by virtue of its advanced radar (which as noted above has excellent range and look-down characteristics to enable the interceptor patrolling at an optimum cruise altitude to detect and engage a range of targets right down to sea level) and the TED (Threat Evaluation Display) for the back-seater. However, the use of data-link equipment also makes the Tornado F.2 admirably suited to operation with AWACS type aircraft, the British contender in this field being the BAe Nimrod AEW.3. The UK at one time toyed with the notion of adopting the Boeing E-3A Sentry (18 of which have been bought by NATO) but was put off the notion by (amongst other factors) the limited capability of the US aircraft's APY-1 surveillance radar, which has proved notably ineffective in overwater conditions. As much as the emphasis in the UK Air Defence Region is placed on interception over the North Sea, the Norwegian Sea and the North Atlantic, such a limitation was clearly undesirable, and the development of a special version of the Nimrod maritime reconnaissance aircraft was put in hand during 1977 with GEC surveillance radar accommodated in bulbous fairings at the nose and tail. An order was placed for 11 Nimrod AEW.3 aircraft converted from Nimrod MR.1 airframes. The specification for the whole Nimrod AEW.3 package was extremely difficult, involving the integration of advanced radar, processing equipment and other electronic equipment into an existing airframe, but offered the promise of un-excelled capability: whereas four of the current and wholly obsolescent Avro Shackleton AEW.2 can cover only spots of the North Sea and southern Norwegian Sea, three Nimrods should be able to provide uninter-rupted cover from the UK to Norway in a strip stretch-ing from West Germany almost to Iceland, with far bet-ter definition than that possible by the E-3A.

Nimrod AEW.3 runs into trouble

Unfortunately, the programme has run into consider-able difficulty with the electronic systems. The first production aircraft was delivered to the Ministry of De-fence in the last week of 1984, but has not been accepted for RAF service because of its problems: the radar has yet to demonstrate the reliability required of a service equipment item, the aircraft has emerged con-siderably overweight (making it impossible to take-off with a full fuel load, with consequent limitations on pat-rol duration) and there are difficulties with heat dissipa-tion. This last has resulted from the need to operate the radar at higher-than-planned power levels to obtain the necessary range: this places extra loads on the gener-ators (leaving them without spare capability) and re-quires the retention of fuel in the wing tanks (as a heat sink) right up to the moment of landing, further reduc-ing operational endurance. There are also problems with signal-processing, and thought is being given to the installation of a larger computer: this would probably be a civilian model 'ruggedised' for military service.

As may well be imagined, these problems have seriously delayed the Nimrod AEW.3 programme, and the type will not become operational until 1987 at the earliest, the base being RAF Waddington. In the mean-time, therefore, the aged Shackleton AEW.2 must sol-dier on with its much upgraded APS-20F surveillance radar. Operated by No.8 Squadron at RAF Los-siemouth, the five available aircraft are presenting monumental maintenance problems, but pending the arrival of the Nimrod AEW.3s these are the only AWACS aircraft available to the RAF.

There can be little doubt but that the interceptor arm is the RAF's weakest link, a situation made the more regrettable by the UK's significance not just for its own sake within the NATO alliance, but as the European terminus for men, materiel and supplies designed to flow across the Atlantic in times of crisis or war. The in-terceptor force of No.11 Group has two main combat types, one of them dating from the 1950s in concept and the other from the early 1960s. Both types have been considerably upgraded over the years, and retain speed and climb performances adequate to the tasks envis-aged. Where they are primarily deficient, therefore, is in the field of electronics and, to a lesser extent, arma-ment.

Long-range Phantom

Longer-range interception is the role of the McDonnell Douglas Phantom, which serves the RAF in three ver-sions, namely the Phantom FG.1, the Phantom FG.2 and the F-4J Phantom. Some 15 examples of this last model were acquired from the US Navy to make up numbers depleted by the Phantoms posted away to the Falklands, and form the strength of No.74 Squadron at RAF Wattisham. The other two Phantom bases are RAF Leuchars, home of Nos 43 and 111 Squadrons, and RAF Coningsby, home of No.29 Squadron and No.228 Operational Conversion Unit. The sixth Phantom unit in No.11 Group's line-up is No.56 Squadron, based at Wattisham with No.29 Squadron. Though still capable, these Phantom aircraft are approaching the ends of their useful first-line lives as a result of expiring air-frame lives and the limited capabilities of their massive liquid-cooled Westinghouse radar equipments.

Short-range interception in the province of the En-glish Electric Lightning, which still possesses climb and speed performance fully up to the threat, but lacks the range, armament and electronics for effective operation against the lastest in Soviet threats, notably the Sukhoi Su-24 'Fencer' interdiction aircraft and the Tupolev Tu-26 'Backfire' variable-geometry supersonic bomber. Armed with a twin 30-mm cannon pack and a mere two IR-homing air-to-air missiles (Red Top weapons carried on the fuselage sides), the Lightning is also hampered by its lack of modern radar, the Airpass system de-

Left: Controversial Airborne Early Warning Nimrod in flight. It is due to replace the ageing Shackleton.

signed by Ferranti in the 1950s having been upgraded subsequently but remaining short-ranged. Thus the Lightning can operate effectively only in conjunction with the GCI (ground-controlled interception) system associated with the UKADR radar network.

The units which operate the Lightning still attest to the type's excellent handling and interception performance, and are based at RAF Binbrook: Nos 5 and 11 Squadrons with a mix of Lightning F.3 and Lightning F.6 aircraft, and the Lightning Training Flight equipped with Lightning T.5 two-seaters. Some 50 Lightnings of all marks remain in service, but will be phased out as the Tornado F.2 enters operational service, when Binbrook will close as a front-line fighter base.

Further defence of the UK is provided by some 72 BAe Hawk T.1A trainers fitted with equipment for two AIM-9L Sidewinder air-to-air missiles. These aircraft are operated by advanced flying and weapons training units 'shadowed' for the point defence of specific targets. The RAF bases themselves are defended by two missile types: Bloodhound SAMS are deployed by No.25 Squadron for the defence of Barkston Heath, Wyton and Wattisham, and by No.85 for Bawdsey, West Raynham and North Coates, while Rapier SAMs are tasked with the protection of Leuchars and Lossiemouth in the hands of Nos 28 and 47 Squadrons, RAF Regiment, respectively.

Europeans collaborate to produce new generation interceptor.

This defence force has very obvious limitations, and the RAF's highest development priority in the near future is a new interceptor to replace the Phantom. BAe is building an ACA (Agile Combat Aircraft) demonstrator to fly in 1986, but hopes are also placed on the proposed EFA (European Fighter Aircraft) mooted by the UK, West Germany, France, Italy and Spain. The EFA notion is attractive for a number of political and economic reasons, and though discussions at ministerial level have during May 1985 finalized an optimum weight of 9500 kg for the new fighter, there are strong possibilities that intractable difficulties between the UK and France will halt the programme as a truly European effort to succeed the highly successful Sepecat Jaguar (UK and France) and Panavia Torado (UK, West Germany and Italy).

The RAF wants a heavier fighter than the French are prepared to consider, and France is adamant that it must have design leadership of the project, so it may well result that France proceeds with the operational development of its Dassault-Breguet Rafale demonstra-

Below: Impression of the Experimental Aircraft Programme Technology demonstrator now under construction at BAe Warton and due to fly in 1986.

tor while the UK pushes on with comparable development of the ACA. West Germany could also undertake the development of an indigenous type, Dornier having produced an attractive concept which might be financially viable after the company's recent take-over by Daimler-Benz.

All the designs feature a blended wing/body and canard foreplanes, and will make extensive use of composite materials, advanced aerodynamics, fly-by-wire flight controls in conjunction with relaxed stability to produce an extremely strong, versatile and manoeuvrable aircraft. Current planning calls for the type or types to enter service in the mid-1990s, but the track records of similar projects indicate that delays will almost certainly follow, suggesting a debut later in that decade.

Harrier GR.5 first flight

The previous No.38 Group of Strike Command has now been fully absorbed into No.1 Group, which is thus responsible for tactical support of British army ground formations. The main offensive strength of this force in the UK is based at RAF Wittering, where No.1 Squadron and No.233 Operational Conversion Unit operate the BAe Harrier GR.3 single-seater and Harrier T.4 two-seater. The Harrier remains a formidable close-support aircraft, but is now beginning to show its age. A Phase 7 update was at first proposed for the Harrier force, but attrition has whittled numbers down to some 70 single-seaters, so it was instead decided to adopt the McDonnell Douglas/BAe Harrier II advanced development, some 60 of which are on order for the RAF with the designation Harrier GR.5.

The first British-assembled Harrier GR.5 flew in May 1985, and it is likely that the production run will be increased to allow eventual replacement of the original Harriers. In comparison with the original all-British model, the Anglo-American development is an altogether more formidable machine: though engine power has been increased slightly, performance and payload capability are much enhanced by reduced structure weight (resulting from extensive use of composite materials in the airframe), a larger wing, improved lift devices, leading-edge root extensions, slotted flaps and zero-scarf nozzles. The effect of these improvements is to boost the payload that can be lifted from a short take-off by more than 6,700 lb. External loads can be carried on one underfuselage and six underwing hardpoints, and the type is cleared from a wide diversity of munitions, which can be delivered with very great accuracy thanks to the provision of a Sea Harrier-type forward fuselage and cockpit (for better fields of vision) allied with a Hughes ARBS (Angle/Rate Bombing System) whose laser/TV target-seeker and tracker is coupled to an advanced Smiths head-up display in the cockpit.

The Harrier GR.5 is due to enter service in 1986, initially with Harrier squadrons in West Germany, though it is expected that the UK-based squadrons will eventually receive later-production examples of the GR.5.

Cont. p. 103

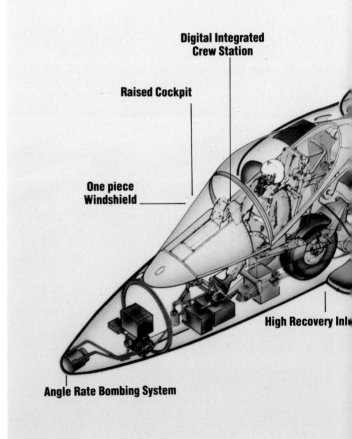

AV-8B/Harrier GR.Mk5

Onboard Oxygen Generating System ___

7,500 lb (3,402 kg) Internal Fuel ___

Digital Integrated Crew Station

Raised Cockpit

One piece Windshield ___

High Recovery Inle

Angle Rate Bombing System

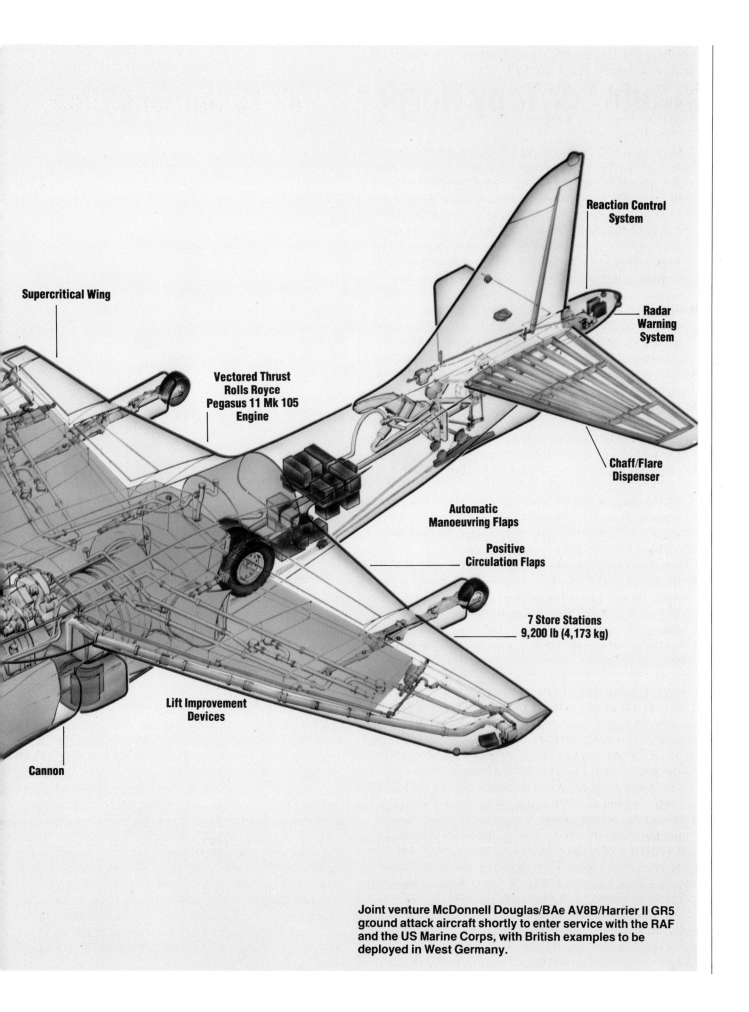

Supercritical Wing

**Vectored Thrust
Rolls Royce
Pegasus 11 Mk 105
Engine**

**Reaction Control
System**

**Radar
Warning
System**

**Chaff/Flare
Dispenser**

**Automatic
Manoeuvring Flaps**

**Positive
Circulation Flaps**

**7 Store Stations
9,200 lb (4,173 kg)**

**Lift Improvement
Devices**

Cannon

Joint venture McDonnell Douglas/BAe AV8B/Harrier II GR5
ground attack aircraft shortly to enter service with the RAF
and the US Marine Corps, with British examples to be
deployed in West Germany.

WHERE ARE THEY NOW?
Sqdn Ldr Tony Harper

Squadron Leader Tony Harper is the Flight Commander of No. 1 Fighter Squadron at RAF Wittering in Northamptonshire, one of the oldest military airfields in the country, with a history going back to the Royal Flying Corps in the years before the First World War. At the age of thirty-four Tony Harper has been in the RAF for nearly fifteen years. He won his pilot's wings in March 1973, in Jet Provosts, and flew Hunters at Chivenor in Devon, and at Wittering during 1974. He stayed on at Wittering to take part in the first Harrier conversion course, changing over from Hunters to the Harrier GR5, basically the same aircraft as the US AV8B, a joint production effort between MacDonald Douglas and British Aerospace. He flew Harriers in Germany until the end of 1977, and then completed a tour as a weapons instructor in Hunters at the Tactical Weapons Unit (TWU) at RAF Lossiemouth in Scotland until 1981. He then went on to start a front-line operational tour at No. 1 Squadron at RAF Wittering, working as an instructor to the conversion unit, training pilots from a variety of aircraft to fly Harriers.

Tony Harper was part of the No. 1 Squadron team that deployed with the task force to retake the Falkland Islands after the Argentine invasion. He left RAF Wittering on May 2nd, 1982. The Harriers flew from St Mawgan to Ascension Island non-stop, a 9¼ hour marathon involving seven mid-air refuellings. They flew three at a time, nine aircraft altogether over a period of three days. From Ascension they continued aboard *Atlantic Conveyor* with six aircraft. Some had been replaced at Ascension by aircraft from Germany, and some remained at Ascension in case of an air threat from Argentina.

From Atlantic Conveyor to Hermes
The Harriers left *Atlantic Conveyor* in the middle of the South Atlantic, three hundred miles from Port Stanley, and about two thousand miles from South Africa, landing on HMS *Hermes*. From *Hermes* Tony Harper and the others flew sorties in support of army units ashore. On May 24th they attacked Stanley airport, and on May 28th supported the Parachute Regiment's attack on Goose Green. The Paras summoned up the Harriers to demonstrate the firepower they had on call, and this forced the surrender at Goose Green. After that the Harriers took part in a series of attacks around and across the Eastern Island. A small airfield was established at Port San Carlos, with two aircraft and a rotation of pilots. After the final surrender of the Argentine force, the squadron moved ashore to Stanley airfield to provide an immediate defence capability against any

Argentine attack from the mainland. They flew continual training sorties, and could be airborne and on station within a few minutes. Resupplies of aircraft and pilots had come in from Ascension in the course of the brief war, to make up losses, making the flight in 8½ hours. Most of the original team returned home on about the 12th of July.

Two months later Tony Harper found himself back at Stanley airfield, and from then on Harriers and pilots from No. 1 Squadron flew out to maintain the alert, usually staying for two to three months at a time. They lived in the most appalling conditions in tents on the airfield itself, in the depths of the Falklands winter, two or three men to a tent. It was bitterly cold, windy and wet all the time, and the pilots had to be within two minutes walk of the aircraft at all times. The Harrier force stayed on, usually six or eight aircraft, though living conditions gradually improved. In June 1985 it was announced that they were finally to be withdrawn as the new airfield neared completion. Tony Harper made the return trip to the Falklands just the once, though other members of the Harrier force completed three and four short tours of up to four months at a time. The Stanley

Above: Falklands veteran Squadron Leader Tony Harper with his Harrier at RAF Wittering in the summer of 1985, prior to their return to Europe. Left: RAF Germany is the primary front line defence posting for the VSTOL Harrier, its ability to operate from limited fields suiting its enemy-harrassment role.

airfield posting was not a popular one, but the flying was excellent. The weather was either very good, with eight-eighths blue skies, or else cloud at thirty feet and gale force winds. The tours also gave the opportunity for practically unrestricted low level exercises, which are impossible in the busy skies and over the heavily populated areas of the UK.

NATO role once more
No. 1 Squadron has now returned to its normal routine of NATO exercises, in Northern Norway, Denmark, Germany, Sardinia, and various detachments in the UK, usually completing 3 or 4 of these exercises per year. In 1984 Tony Harper took part in exercises in Norway in March, Denmark in September, and Sardinia in November. In Norway the squadron was deployed in support of land forces near the north cape. British forces are usually on manoeuvres there during winter months, and there is often a multinational force present of NATO members such as Canada and Belgium. "In Norway we operate from a civilian airfield called Tromso, which is normally snow and ice-covered while we're there. These are always winter exercises – there's no point in

going there otherwise. We do some weapons practice and close air support training sorties. Close air support is direct support of forces on the ground, airborne artillery if you like. The conditions provide quite a lot of problems. Flying the aircraft off and landing on the snow and ice are difficult. You have problems keeping the aircraft straight on take-off, and you have to land at very low speeds so that once you're on the ground you can physically stop before the end of the runway. The cold weather affects the performance of the engine. Because the Harrier engine operates fairly near to its performance limit a lot of the time, a difference in outside air temperature can incur various atmospheric pressure changes within the engine. The automatic limiting system on the engine can't always cope, so you have to manually control it. The cold can induce a tendency for the engine to surge. The other problems associated with flying in snow and ice are to do with low flying. In conditions of white ground and white sky you don't get a clear horizon definition, and it's very easy to lose your perception of height over the ground. You can fly into the ground if you're not careful. Nearly all the flying is by sight rather than instruments. There are lots of small pine forests, with trees that may be no more than five or six feet tall, but they actually look the same as fifty foot trees. If you're looking at something like that to judge your distance off, then you lose your perspective. The weather conditions out there are interesting too. It's either nice and blue, classic ice-field conditions, or else it's chucking down snow like nobody's business. So you have to learn to judge which bits you can use and which you can't. You obviously can't do a ground attack in a snowstorm. You're forced onto your instruments, and have to go up, so you're out of operation in fact. The rate of change of things in a Harrier is very fast. You're going at seven miles a minute, and weather conditions can change so quickly that you have to be a fairly fine judge of what's coming up. With the younger, inexperienced guys, the more training we can give them in those sorts of conditions, the better."

Dissimilar Air Combat Training

Norway is also used for the practice of Dissimilar Air Combat Training, which is dog-fighting with the aircraft of other NATO forces, such as the US F15s and F16s, the Norwegians' F5s, and British Jaguars. A ground radar control unit oversees the take-off and positioning of the 'jousting' aircraft, which then approach one another head on at different altitudes, and at speeds up to 600 knots. After making visual contact – the Harriers have no airborne radar – the aim is to manoeuvre into a position where a simulated weapons kill can be made. For a guns kill the aircraft have to be within five hundred yards of each other. Winners are decided by an analysis of gunsight camera films on the ground. The Demark exercises are similar to those in Norway, though the terrain is a lot flatter, with more water and less snow.

Sardinia is used as the standard weapons training camp for front-line squadrons. For three weeks No. 1 Squadron dropped bombs on the Sardinian ranges, after having deployed down to Sardinia using air to air refuelling (AAR). The first task was to convert from 'ferry fit' to 'weapons fit', a matter of exchanging fuel probes and tanks for weapon fitments. A typical training run could involve taking off and transiting in fours to the range. All movements are rigidly controlled by the Italians. Only one type of aircraft is allowed on the range at any one time, though the base is quadrinational, with aircraft from Italy, Germany, the UK and the USA. The first run attack might be a low level bombing run, followed by four further bomb attacks. This might then be followed by half a dozen rocket attacks, and then four strafing attacks with the 30 mm cannon.

New tactics have developed as a result of the Falkland Islands experience, including lower attack heights, and the firing of rockets from the level as well as during dives. It was known that this was feasible, and the tactics were put into operational use in the Falklands, and have been incorporated into the training schedules.

Above: Jaguar of 2 Squadron, RAF Germany. Despite the relative age of the type, they may remain in service ten or more years. Jaguars, along with other NATO aircraft, provide 'enemy' simulation for Dissimilar combat training.

Another new technique not used prior to the Falklands is the Harriers' new capability of delivering laser-guided bombs. This was used for the first time in the Falklands, allowing an amazing degree of accuracy, with bombs delivered to within plus or minus three feet of the target at a range of two to three miles.

Harriers and Carriers

UK manoeuvres in the past year have included an annual exercise in which half a dozen RAF Harriers and their crews spend a week flying from naval aircraft carriers. This enables new aircrews to get experience in carrier take-offs and landings, as well as carrying out combat training against Sea Harriers, and practising land support roles from the sea. In 1984 HMS *Invincible* was the base for the week's exercise, and the Harriers of No. 1 Squadron flew in support of an army exercise in Devon and Cornwall.

Tony Harper, like the other Harrier pilots at RAF Wittering, flies up to 25 hours a month. That involves flights between one and three times a week, with a flight at least once a day in good weather. A typical day's trip could consist of a planning meeting at 2 MP, followed by a 3.30 PM take-off. A radar-controlled outward journey might consist of a westward leg at 35,000 feet, followed by low level exercises around Anglesey and North Wales, returning once more at 35,000 feet under the radar control of the joint civilian/services unit at West Drayton near London Airport. Landing would be at 4.30 PM, after a minimum exercise of 2½ hours, followed by a half-hour debrief.

In the spring of 1985 Flight Lieutenant Tony Harper was promoted to Squadron Leader, and became Squadron Commander of No. 1 Squadron, where he has been flying Harriers on and off since their introduction to the RAF over a decade ago.

Jaguar still a potent aircraft

Also based in the UK are four units equipped with the Jaguar GR.1 single-seater and Jaguar T.2 two-seat operational trainer. Based at RAF Coltishall are Nos 6, 41 and 54 Squadrons: the first and last are conventional strike squadrons, while No. 41 is a dedicated tactical reconnaissance unit, its Jaguars carrying a BAe reconnaissance pod under the fuselage. The last UK-based Jaguar unit is No. 226 Operational Conversion Unit, which is located at Lossiemouth in Scotland.

Though its design dates from the early 1960s, the Jaguar is still a potent tactical aircraft with guided weapons and with free-fall conventional or nuclear bombs. Right from the beginning of the programme the RAF required the type to have a digital navigation and weapon-aiming system (NAVWAS), but this is now one of the type's weaker points, and the NAVWAS is now being replaced by the Ferranti FIN 1064 digital inertial navigation and weapon-aiming system. And despite the age of the type there is still plenty of development potential in the Jaguar, though this remains largely unexplored in operational versions for lack of funding. Current RAF thinking is veering towards a variant of the proposed EFA as a Jaguar replacement in the mid-1990s, though the Jaguar could perhaps offer greater possibilities in this sphere. Combined with the new nav/attack system and an updated cockpit, the Jaguar's ability to carry a larger wing would enable it to carry more than its current 10,500-lb attack load, whose delivery accuracy is ensured by the nav/attack system and the inbuilt laser ranger and marked-target seeker in the nose. The French have produced a version of the Jaguar with Agave radar in the nose, and provision of such equipment in British Jaguars, together with wingtip rails for close-range air-to-air missiles, would keep the Jaguar in the forefront of the RAF's inventory as a dual-role aircraft right up to the end of the century.

Rotary-wing support for the army in the UK is also the responsibility of No. 1 Group from bases at RAF Odiham and RAF Leconfield. At the former are located Nos 7 and 33 Squadrons, together with No. 240 Operational Conversion Unit. No. 7 Squadron flies Boeing Vertol Chinook HC.1 heavy-lift helicopters, No. 33 Squadron operates Aerospatiale Puma HC.1 medium-lift tactical helicopters, and No. 240 OCU is the conversion unit for the Chinook, Puma and Westland Wessex. This last type is deployed operationally at Leconfield, the home of No. 72 Squadron.

Maritime reconnaissance Nimrod still in front

The maritime assets of Strike Command are allocated to No. 18 Group, which is responsible for the maritime reconnaissance and strike, anti-submarine warfare and search-and-rescue roles round the UK. For the maritime reconnaissance and longer-range anti-submarine

Right: An RAF Flying Officer Harrier pilot in full flying kit, including partial pressure suit and 'bone dome'.

roles the primary weapon is the BAe Nimrod MR.2, a magnificent platform fully comparable with any similar aircraft anywhere in the world. The four operational squadrons with this type are Nos 42, 120, 201 and 206 based at RAF St Mawgan and RAF Kinloss, and these are supported by the efforts of No.236 Operational Conversion Unit. Able to transit at high speeds to their patrol areas, the Nimrod MR.2s can then shut down two of their four turbofans and cruise at low speed for long periods as they search for enemy submarines and surface vessels with radar, sonobuoy and MAD (magnetic anomaly detection) equipment, whose inputs are correlated by an onboard data-processing system and presented to the tactical navigator in the form of an attack plot suitable for the Nimrod's weapons (homing torpedoes, depth charges and, in some instances, anti-ship missiles). It is also likely that in time of war the Nimrods would be armed with Sidewinder air-to-air missiles for self defence. The Nimrod MR.2 also has data-link equipment so that it can communicate complex information in real time to other British or allied units, both in the air and on the surface of the sea.

Though the Nimrod has an anti-ship capability, this is limited by the tactical undesirability of hazarding so expensive and vulnerable an aircraft close to hostile air defences. It is likely, therefore, that attacks on surface vessels would be entrusted to the BAe Buccaneer S.2 strike aircraft of Nos 12 and 208 Squadrons. Based at Lossiemouth, these two operational squadrons are supported at the same base by No.237 Operational Conversion Unit, the three units mustering some 50 aircraft between them. Now decidedly elderly, the Buccaneer has nonetheless proved itself to be one of the best aircraft in the RAF inventory despite the service's scepticism when it inherited the type from the Fleet Air Arm. But so effective is the Buccaneer in the long-range sea-level strike role that the RAF would now dearly like to receive more of the type, which has begun to suffer from airframe problems as a result of age. Survivors are shortly be to upgraded electronically for the high-threat scenario of the present, and a new weapon for the type is the BAe Sea Eagle sea-skimming anti-ship missile.

Below: RAF VC10 tanker aircraft. These ageing passenger jets are finding a new lease of life with Strike Command's transport fleet, based at Brize Norton.

Elderly Canberra still in service

No.18 Group is also tasked with the RAF's photo-reconnaissance, electronic reconnaissance and electronic warfare roles. The main aircraft type in these roles is the obsolescent English Electric Canberra, which is flown by four units: No.1 Photographic Reconnaissance Unit with the Canberra PR.9, No.100 Squadron with a mixed bag for target facilities use, No.360 with Canberra T.17s for ECM training, and No.231 Operational Conversion Unit. These are all based at RAF Wyton, but are currently operating from the nearby US Air Force base at Alconbury while Wyton's runways are resurfaced. A sister squadron, and one of the most highly classified in RAF service, is No.51 Squadron which operates three Nimrod R.1 aircraft in the electronic intelligence role. There can be no denial of the Canberra's need for rapid replacement, and the RAF is currently assessing civilian types for off-the-shelf purchase and subsequent conversion to the roles now undertaken by the Canberras.

Other electronic roles are performed from RAF Benson by the specialist No.115 Squadron, which flies nine Hawker Siddeley Andover aircraft (seven E.3s and two C.1s) for the essential navaid and radar calibration task. Also at Benson is The Queen's Flight. This currently operates three Andover CC.2s and two Wessex HCC.4s, though a welcome injection of modernity will result from the delivery in 1986 of two BAe 146 C.1 four-turbofan transports.

Transport fleet of Strike Command

Strike Command is responsible additionally for the RAF's transport fleet, based at RAF Brize Norton and RAF Lyneham. Brize Norton is the home for the 13 VC10 C.1s of No.10 Squadron and the TriStar C.1s of No.216 Squadron, while Lyneham is the location of the Hercules Wing (Nos 24, 30, 47 and 70 Squadrons, plus No.242 Operational Conversion Unit). Thirty of the 60 aircraft are being converted to Hercules C.3 stretched configuration equivalent to the C-130H-30, and of the total 22 are fitted as tanker or receiver aircraft (16 Hercules C.1/3Ps and six Hercules C.1Ks) for operation by Nos 47 and 70 Squadrons.

Coastal search-and-rescue is undertaken by Strike Command helicopters, notably the Wessex HC.2s and Sea King HAR.3s of Nos 22 and 202 Squadrons, which operate as detached flight at tactical locations round the coasts of the UK.

Strike Command exercises control over a number of overseas detachments. The most important of these at present is that in the Falkland Islands, while other detachments are No.28 Squadron in Hong Kong with Wessex helicopters, No.48 Squadron at Akrotiri with Wessex HCC.5s, and in Belize a force comprising No.1417 Flight with Harrier GR.3s and No.1563 Flight with Puma HC.1s.

Though controlled administratively by Strike Command, the vital assets of RAF Germany are run operationally by the 2nd Allied Tactical Air Force. RAF Germany has four bases: Gutersloh, Wildenrath, Laarbruch and Bruggen. At Gutersloh are found the command's two Harrier close-support squadrons (Nos 3 and 4), which will begin to receive Harrier GR.5s during 1986. Though most of the squadrons' permanent facilities are located at Gutersloh, the squadrons are designed to disperse to extemporized airstrips in time of crisis, and so escape the almost certain destruction that will be rained upon squadrons unable to deploy away from lengthy fixed runways. Wildenrath is home to a pair of Phantom air-defence squadrons, Nos 19 and 92. Laarbruch was the home of RAF Germany's Buccaneer squadrons, but these two units (Nos 15 and 16 Squadrons) have recently converted to the Tornado GR.1. And at Bruggen are found five squadrons, all equipped until recently with the Jaguar: No.31 Squadron has converted to the Tornado GR.1, with Nos 14, 17 and 2) following in 1985 and 1986, and the reconnaissance-tasked No.11 Squadron completing the wing in 1987.

Vital role of helicopters

These are RAF Germany's primary combat assets, but army support in this crucial theatre means that the command is also well furnished with helicopters, Nos 18 and 23) Squadrons operating Chinook HC.1s and Puma HC.1s respectively from Gutersloh. Liaison is the task of No.60 Squadron at Wildenrath with seven ancient Hunting Pembroke CC.1s. Finally, airfield defence of these key bases is undertaken by the RAF Regiment with Rapier SAMs: No.63 Squadron for Gutersloh, No.16 Squadron for Wildenrath, No.26 Squadron for Laarbruch and No.37 Squadron for Bruggen.

Support Command in the UK is responsible for all back-up for the operational groups, and also undertakes flying training. There are 13 air experience flights, 16 university air squadrons, one flying selection squadron, and a number of flying training schools with a variety of equipment for all levels of flying training. Standard equipment at the moment are the BAe Bulldog and the BAe Jet Provost, though this latter is to be replaced from 1987 by Brazilian-designed Embraer Tucano aircraft produced under licence by Shorts. The initial order is for 130 aircraft, and the politically motivated decision for this type was taken in 1985 against the wishes of the RAF itself, which preferred the Swiss-designed Pilatus PC-9 development of the PC-7 Turbo Trainer. After initial training aircrew move on to the BAe Dominie T.1 (navigator training), the BAe Jetstream T.1 (multiengine training) or the BAe Hawk T.1 (advanced operational training). The last type is in service with No.1 Tactical Weapons Unit at Brawdy and No.2 TWU at Chivenor, both controlled by No.11 Group. Rotary-wing training is the province of the Central Flying School at Shawbury.

Fleet Air Arm riding high

Naval air power is again in the hands of the Fleet Air

Above: Medium-life Puma of RAF Germany. These helicopters provide support for the Rhine army and are based at Gutersloh.

Arm, which is enjoying a useful renaissance after the dire days of the 1970s when the Royal Navy's conventional aircraft-carriers were phased out of service. The Falklands War confirmed naval belief that fixed-wing air power was essential for the success of maritime operations, and in the circumstances the decision that the UK should retain all three 'Invincible' class light aircraft-carriers was entirely sensible. Not so sensible, however, has been the Royal Navy's decision that the three carriers should share only two carrier air groups as one carrier is always being refitted. The trouble with this apparently logical decision is that air group personnel and aircraft thus have to serve long hours, with adverse effects on both.

The FAA's fixed-wing strength lies with a force of 34 BAe Sea Harrier FRS.1 aircraft, with another 23 aircraft on order. The Sea Harrier proved itself an admirable aircraft in the Falklands War, but clearly had deficiencies that would be fatal in the context of a war against Warsaw Pact forces. The chief of these failings was the type's limited-capability Ferranti Blue Fox radar and IR-homing short-range Sidewinder missiles. The Sea Harrier is thus to receive a mid-life update to FRS.2 standard with coherent pulse-Doppler Ferranti Sea Vixen radar to provide a longer-range look-down capability, and AIM-120 AMRRAM air-to-air missiles for medium-range engagement of enemy aircraft. Other improvements will be the provision of a Guardian radar-warning receiver and the Joint Tactical Information Dis-

tribution System to provide secure voice and data links. Combined with other improvements, this will make the FAA's Sea Harrier force considerably more effective. Current operators of the Sea Harrier FRS.1 are the operational Nos 800 and 801 Squadrons, and the HQ and training No.899 Squadron, all shore-based at RNAS Yeovilton.

Need for airborne early warning

The Falklands War revealed the extreme gravity of the tactical situation into which naval forces could be placed when operating without AWACS support, and to remedy this situation a notion of the 1960s has been revived to produce the Westland Sea King AEW, to total eight conversions fitted with Thorn-EMI Searchwater radar in a large radome on the starboard side of the fuselage. No.824 Squadron at RNAS Culdrose was the original operator of Sea King AEWs, but No.849 Squadron has been re-formed at the same base to undertake the RN airborne early warning role, deploying flights of two helicopters on ships as necessary.

Helicopters form the bulk of the FAA's assets: the two most important of these types are the Westland Sea King anti-submarine helicopter, and the Westland Lynx light anti-submarine and anti-ship helicopter. The Sea Kings are all now of HAS.5 standard with Plessey

Above: Royal Navy Lynx helicopter releases lightweight torpedo during Atlantic trials. Right: Heavy-lift Chinook of 18 Squadron RAF Germany transporting truck and Rapier missile launcher.

Type 195 dunking sonar and MEL Sea Searcher search radar, and are designed for semi-autonomous anti-submarine operations from the Royal Navy's larger warships. The Lynxes are of the HAS.2 and HAS.3 marks, and though fitted with Bendix ASQ-13 dunking sonar and provision for anti-submarine weapons, are more commonly used from smaller warships for anti-ship work with a quarter of Sea Skua sea-skimming missiles launched on the data provided by the Ferranti Sea Spray search and tracking radar. Though the Sea King is intended to be replaced by the Anglo-Italian EH.101 helicopter in the 1990s, the type will remain in service thereafter and receive electronic and systems updates. There appears to be no replacement in sight for the excellent little Lynx, and the type will certainly soldier on in successively improved variants. Sea King units are Nos 706, 810, 814, 819, 820, 824 and 826 Squadrons, while the Lynx operator is No.815 Squadron, which provides flights to ships as necessary.

For assault transport of the Royal Marine Commandos, the FAA operates the Wessex HU.5 with No.845 Squadrons, and the Westland Commando HC.4 with Nos 707 (part) and 846 Squadrons, with another squadron forming in 1985. These units are based at Yeovil-

Above: Cockpit of Rediffusion's Full Mission Navy Lynx Simulator with night/dusk Computer Generated Image visual display, currently in service with the Royal Navy at RNAS Portland.

Left: Impression of EH101 helicopter, currently under development by Westland and Agusta of Italy.

ton, and more Wessex HU.5s are operated from Culdrose and Portland by Nos 707 (part), 771 and 772 Squadrons for search-and-rescue and training duties. Most of the Wessexes will have gone into retirement by 1986. Other FAA helicopters are the Westland Wasp HAS.1 for anti-ship and survey work from small vessels, and the Gazelle HT.1 for training with No.705 Squadron at Culdrose. Jetsteam T.2 and T.3 aircraft are used for observer training by No.750 Squadron, while the civilian-operated Fleet Requirements and Air Direc-

Above: British Army Lynx helicopter firing TOW anti-tank missile. The Army Aviation Corps operates over 300 helicopters and fixed wing aircraft in a variety of support and utility roles.

tion Unit at Yeovilton runs a miscellany of fixed-wing types for its diverse tasks.

Army Aviation Corps

The Army Aviation Corps is an independent formation within the British army, and operates about 300 helicopters for a variety of army roles. The AAC also musters some 35 fixed-wing aircraft for the utility and training roles. The aircraft are 10 de Havilland Canada Beaver STOL transports, 24 de Havilland Chipmunk trainers, and one Britten-Norman Islander being used for the trials associated with the CASTOR (Corps Airborne STand-Off Radar) programme.

The helicopters in greatest use are the Gazelle liaison type, the Lynx AH.1 anti-tank and utility type, and the Westland Scout AH.1 anti-tank type. There are also some 18 Aerospatiale Alouette IIIs for liaison. The organization of the AAC is into regiments, each consisting of two squadrons: one flies reconnaissance with the Gazelle, and the other operates in the anti-tank role with either the AS.11-armed Scout or the far more formidable TOW-armed Lynx. The AAC's main strength is in West Germany for the support of the BAOR: headquartered at Detmold, No.1 Wing has under command the 1st Regiment (Nos 651 and 661 Squadrons at Hildesheim), the 2nd Regiment (Nos 654 and 664 Squadrons at Bunde and Munster respectively), the 3rd Regiment (Nos 653 and 663 Squadrons at Soest), the 4th Regiment (Nos 659 and 669 Squadrons at Minden), and the 9th Regiment as the HQ unit (Nos 659 and 669 Squadrons at Detmold). Two Gazelle flights are located in Germany, in the forms of No.7 Flight in Berlin and No.12 Flight at Wildenrath. Other AAC assets are located in the UK, Hong Kong (No.660 Squadron with Scouts), Belize, Cyprus and Canada.

For the future the army is assessing the need for a dedicated anti-tank helicopter, perhaps the Agusta A 129. The army also realizes the need for an anti-helicopter helicopter, to escort anti-tank and utility transport helicopter, and conducted some useful trials during Operation 'Lionheart' in West Germany during the September 1984 NATO exercise in Europe.

Chapter 6

SEA WAR: SUBMARINE SERVICE

A personal account of what the world underwater means to the men who must learn to fight and survive in it, often for several months at a time, without sight of land or even sea, without contact from home and almost no privacy. Plus the constant threat of an unseen enemy.

Royal Navy nuclear-powered hunter-killer SSN submarine of the *Swiftsure* class approaches Faslane.

When you join up they give you all sorts of information about the navy, and submarines is one of the things you get a lecture about – it still happens today. Of course when you're that age, 17, 18, you say, 'Oh, I'd be quite happy to put my name down for that' and a lot of us did. It's just one of the options. In 1960 it wasn't such a big deal, because the submarine world was a lot smaller. So, somewhere on my papers it said, This man volunteers for submarines. By 1967 I'd completely forgotten about signing to say I was willing to go into subs. So receiving a draft order to proceed to HMS Dolphin for submarine training was something of a shock." Thus begins many a submariners story.

HMS Dolphin is the submarine training establishment at Portsmouth, and the home of the 1st Submarine Squadron. Everyone who joins submarines goes to Dolphin for their submarine training. The 1st Squadron is a totally conventional patrol submarine squadron, equipped with diesel-powered 'O' and 'P' boats. The 2nd Submarine Squadron is based at Plymouth, made up of nuclear powered hunter-killer submarines. The bulk of these are Swiftsure class, and there are also the first of the Trafalgar class to be deployed. Up at Faslane in Scotland is the 3rd Submarine Squadron, consisting mainly of nuclear powered submarines, and Faslane is also the home of the 10th Submarine Squadron, the Polaris squadron.

Bob Evans did his basic sub training at HMS Dolphin, and was then 'nominated' for Polaris training. At Faslane he attended a 4 month course on the Polaris weapons system, and was then seconded to the Vickers company in Barrow in Furness to help build the new Polaris subs. 'Resolution' was already in the water, and Bob Evans joined 'Repulse'. She was still on the slips, not yet launched, when the thirty officers and senior ratings joined the Vickers engineering staff. Everything had to be learned as they went along. They were aboard, learning, fitting, and drawing up the instruction manuals for future engineers for eighteen months before the sea trials.

Contrary to popular belief service in the submarines is not a voluntary option these days. Those picked by the navy go for sub training after basic training, and maybe even after a spell aboard a conventional surface vessel.

"Someone coming in stright off the street would go to HMS Raleigh down at Tor Point in Cornwall. It's the new entry training establishment for all ratings joining the navy. That includes WRNS as well now – everyone goes there. How long you spend at Raleigh depends on what branch you are going into. The bulk of the lads spend 6 to 8 weeks there training, and then go off for their part 2 training, which is the trade training. The first 8 weeks is identical for all the ratings."

Although a rating cannot refuse to go for sub training, he can indicate that that is what he would like to do, though nothing is guaranteed.

Above: *Porpoise* class diesel-electric powered submarine, HMS *Walrus*, now being phased out of service. *Porpoise* class boats preceded the later diesel-electric *Oberon* class, and carried a complement of seventy officers and ratings.

"The submarine service is a lot bigger than when I joined, so a higher percentage are inevitably going to join submarines whether they volunteer or not. The bottom line in the navy is that when you sign on you are informed that you are liable, if the service requires, to do service in submarines. In fact a far higher percentage are tied up in submarines because it's expanded so much. Nowadays I see whole classes going into submarines, whereas when I oined the odd man in the odd class was going in. Of course subs are much bigger now, and require bigger crews. The ordinary conventional submarine's got a crew of around sixty, sixty-five. Compare that with a 'bomber' (Polaris) that's running around these days with about a hundred and fifty on board."

T Class replacing Polaris

"The latest submarines being built are the T Class. They're poles apart from their predecessors. The Polaris is a twenty year old model. It's like cars. You

can't compare them. Also you're almost getting to the point where submarines in the same class are different. Sometimes quite radically different. For instance, when a new communications system comes in, the one that's on the slip gets it. It's predecessors will get it possibly on the next refit."

The man from basic training goes for his part 2. If he want's to be an Electrical Mechanic like Bob Evans he'll go to Collingwood. An electrical rating is called a 'Greenie' – after the colour green used to denote earth in electrical wiring. (Mechanical ratings are known as 'clankies'). At Collingwood the rating does basic electrical training, at the end of which he either goes to sea in general service, or he may find himself going to HMS Dolphin to commence submarine training. The first thing they do is a general submarine course, wheatever their trade. At the end of the general course he is streamed into whichever area he's going into.

"For instance, if he's going into a conventional sub, a patrol sub, he'll do the relevant course for that type of submarine. The general course will have talked about patrol, fleet and Polaris subs. He'll then go into the specialised side, of an 'O' boat, 'S' boat, 'T' boat, or whatever, depending on what the equipment is he's going to work on. So these are specialist equipment courses. There's even more specialisation these days of course. 25 years ago an electrical engineer was just an electrical engineer, nowadays he's an engineer who already

Below: HMS *Otus*, an *Oberon* class patrol submarine under way. The class are armed with six 21 inch main bow tubes, and two stern-firing anti-submarine tubes for a total 24 torpedoes.

Above left: USS *Michigan* (SSBN-727) *Ohio*-class Trident missile submarine under construction for the US Navy at Groton in Connecticut. Trident has been chosen as the Polaris strategic deterrent for the Royal Navy. Below left: USS *Michigan* undergoing sea trials in 1983 begins a dive. Above: Forward view aboard USS *Ohio*, class lead ship, showing open Trident C-4 missile launch tubes. The missiles are removed for servicing after patrols. Patrols currently last seventy days, with 25 day refit periods in between.

knows about computers. You never catch up. When they complete their specialist courses they either go to that sub, or they might find themselves in Faslane, or Devonport or Dolphin waiting to pick up a submarine. If the chap he's going to relieve isn't due off the boat for another few months, the rating will go and work in the workshops or something until he picks up the submarine."

Part 3

The newly qualifed rating, having completed his specialist training, and perhaps having waited for the man he is replacing to move on, now joins his first submarine. "The first thing he's going to do when he gets aboard is what they call a Part 3. This is only ever done aboard the sub. He will now spend a considerable amount of time learning that submarine. All systems – everything on board. He's on board as part of the crew, but he's still under training. But he will be expected to carry out tasks at the same time. Though he'll have to pass boards (exams) before they'll allow him to touch

anything. That first three months is a hard time to get through. Hopefully you sort out the wheat from the chaff at this stage of the game. The new rating automatically goes under the wing of the Chief in charge of that particular section. The chief will allot a watch to him. The chap in charge of the watch may be a PO or a leading hand. Or he might be another chief (CPO).

"There's a great variety of watches. The new rating on his first tour will be at sea for 18 months at least, possibly stretching out to 30 months. He will be part of that ship's company for a minimum of 18 months, unless it goes for refit. The maximum is supposed to be for 30 months. Mind you, I was on Repulse for nearly seven years. In the course of the first tour, if the new man doesn't get through his Part 3 in the first three months, then he'll get kicked around a bit. Everyone on board will bend over backwards to help him, mind, because it's in everybody's interest that he knows what he's doing. He may be the guy who's standing near an important valve when something goes wrong. Everyone does watches, including the new lad. He can only get through his Part 3 book when he's off watch. That three months he's not going to have a lot of time at all. He's watchkeeping, he's doing his Part 3. At the end of it he's going to do a written exam and an oral exam with the first Lieutenant of the submarine. The oral will quite literally be a 'walking through the boat' oral. Not sitting across a desk. He'll ask what's this, what's that, and if you can't come out with the answers, then you've failed. In which case your submarine pay disappears. They give it to you after you've completed your basic

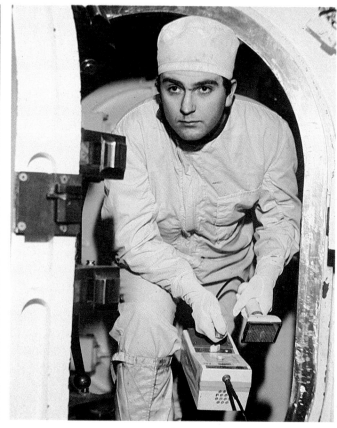

Above: Britain's independent nuclear deterrent is maintained at present by *Resolution* class nuclear-powered ballistic-missile submarines carrying Polaris UGM-27C A-3 underwater missiles: Navigator checking charts in control room of HMS *Repulse*. Right: Regular checks are made on nuclear-powered boats by Geiger counter to guard against radiation leaks. Above right: Ratings operating listening equipment in the Sound Room aboard HMS *Resolution*. As with other navies' SSBNs, *Resolution* class boats have two crews on rotation (known as port and starboard) – one at sea and one on shore preparing to take over the submarine when the others return from patrol, to make fullest use of the time available. Far right: HMS *Resolution* passes beneath the Forth road bridge in Scotland.

training, but at that stage it's a gift. In that first three months you're expected to qualify to wear the dolphins. If you don't, they might give you another 4 weeks. Part three is a familiarisation course. Electricians have to understand mechanical things. Chefs have to understand electrics. Of course the novice is also learning his actual job on board at the same time. The man is taking the boards for his particular specialisation at the same time. If you get someone who doesn't really put himself out, (and everyone will notice), and he fails, then he can say goodbye to his submarine pay. In extreme cases he will see the captain, and he will be landed, and he will be sent back to general service."

The Submarine Fleet

The Royal Navy's Fleet is composed of three surface-vessel flotillas, a four-squadron Mine Countermeasures Command and the Submarine Command, of which the latter is the most secret and, to many (submariners themselves in particular) the most elite. At present, Submarine Command comprises four squadrons, with a current operating total of 28 vessels.

Not all submarines are alike, however, and three distinct types – apart from the various classes – are deployed in widely differing roles as part of Britain 's independent nuclear deterrent, and the more technical business of the navy's NATO responsibility in keeping the sea lanes of the North Atlantic free of Soviet activity in the event of a NATO-Warsaw Pact war.

The oldest – and currently most numerous-type are the diesel-electric *Oberon* and *Porpoise* class patrol submarines, known by the abbreviation SSKs. These, like their World War II forebears, are battery-powered when submerged with a maximum speed of about 20 knots and rely on diesel-engine generators to recharge the batteries either while surface-running, or via 'snort' tubes which can be raised while underwater to scoop air for the engines and thus reduce the risk of detection by enemy observers. Harder to detect than the larger nuclear-powered submarines, the SSKs still make up a

Harpoon anti-ship missile

Guidance

Warhead

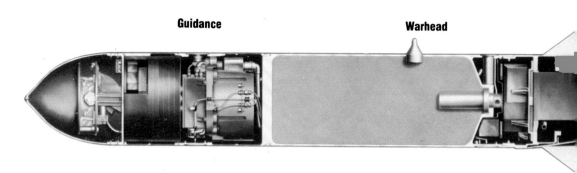

Royal Navy Trident Missile Submarine

This conjectural diagram is based upon the latest British submarine-building practices, allowing for the increased volume of the C-4 Trident II missile system.

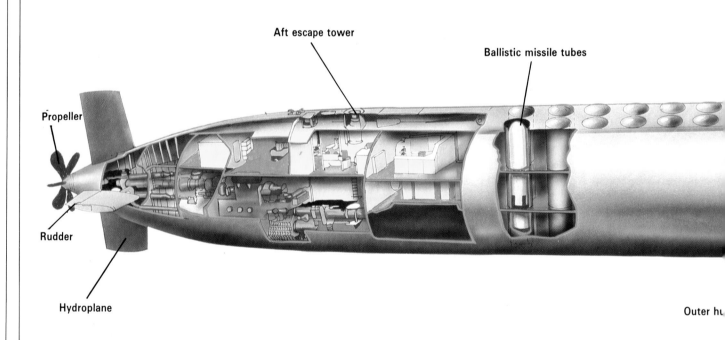

Aft escape tower

Ballistic missile tubes

Propeller

Rudder

Hydroplane

Outer hu

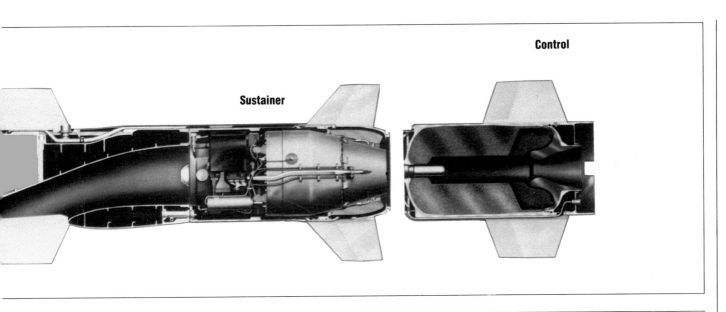

Sustainer

Control

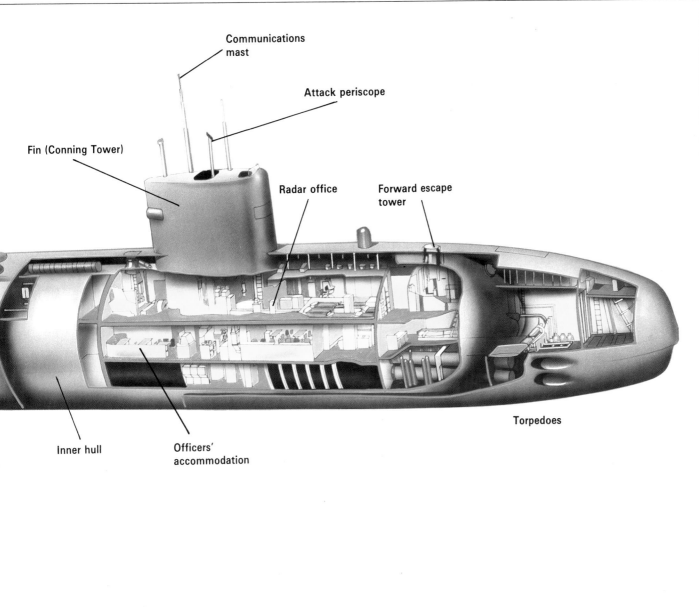

Communications
mast

Attack periscope

Fin (Conning Tower)

Radar office

Forward escape
tower

Torpedoes

Inner hull

Officers'
accommodation

significant part of the Command and are used for a variety of purposes including training, minelaying, operations with special forces like the Special Boat Section or SAS, onshore/offshore patrol duties and, in the case of Poseidon especially, sinking enemy shipping.

SSNs and SSBNs

Nuclear-powered Fleet submarines currently form the backbone of the Command, and break down into three classes: *Valiant, Swiftsure* and *Trafalgar*. These are the anti-submarine hunter-killers, deployed in the Atlantic to protect supply lines from enemy torpedoes. The first of these vessels was *Valiant,* now coming to the end of her service, and the most recent *Trafalgar,* the first of several in the class, which was commissioned in 1984. Armed with Tigerfish torpedoes and the long-range Sub-Harpoon anti-ship missile, SSNs are able to operate for extended periods without surfacing – as much as 2 months at a time – and independently of covert shore-based support facilities. Much larger than the SSKs, hunter-killers carry a complement of over a hundred officers and men and are much more spacious,

Cont. p. 124

Right: Control room of HMS *Sovereign* manned for Diving Stations. Below right: Crewmen aboard another *Swiftsure* class SSN, HMS *Splendid*, relax while off duty in the messroom. Far right, above: HMS *Warspite* surfacing off Faslane is armed with homing torpedoes and four Sub Harpoon missiles. Below: Tigerfish homing torpedo.

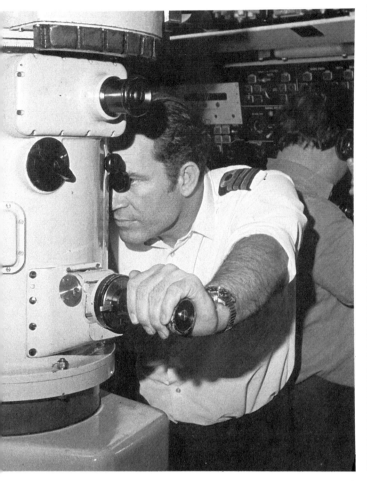

ONE WHO WAS THERE
Lt Paul Crudgington, RNAS

Lieutenant Paul Crudgington flies Sea King helicopters in 706 Naval Air Squadron, based at Culdrose, a sprawling, windswept camp and airfield in the far south west of Cornwall, near the Lizard. For all its remote site, Culdrose is the busiest helicopter station in Europe, and the air is constantly ruptured by the dark, clattering shapes of the Sea Kings taking off and landing. RNAS helicopters provide the airborne element in the painstaking task of locating enemy submarines – Britain's primary NATO role in the North Atlantic.

Paul Crudgington joined the Navy at the age of twenty-one, over twelve years ago. He flew for five years as an observer, and then retrained as a pilot. The road to the Sea King was long and varied. Starting at the officer training school at Dartmouth at the beginning of his service, he first of all did a small amount of Chipmunk flying, before going for the first of many stints at Culdrose. His first full-time flying training was with 750 Squadron at Culdrose, on Sea Princes, the old twin-engined piston aircraft that were the training forerunners to the Jetstreams used today. This was followed by his first helicopter training in Wessex helicopters at Portland on 737 Squadron. After four months he went to 706 Squadron and its Sea Kings for the first time. In the ensuing years, still an observer at this time, he carried out two front-line tours with operational, sea-based squadrons. Training squadrons, such as 706, are known as second-line squadrons.

In 1978 he applied for and began pilot-training, starting with small Bulldog trainers, at RAF Leeming in Yorkshire. For helicopter pilot training he returned once again to Culdrose, to 705 Squadron, where he started out on Gazelles, which are still the Navy's training helicopter. He received his pilot's wings in August 1980, and went on to learn operational piloting in the Sea Kings of 706 Squadron.

Falklands crisis cuts short leave

Like many other servicemen, Paul Crudgington was on Easter leave when the Falklands crisis occurred. For two years he had been flying Sea Kings with 826 Squadron, based on HMS Hermes when at sea, and at Culdrose when shorebound. At that time 826 was a standard Anti Submarine Warfare (ASW) squadron of nine or ten aircraft, and still is a part of the ASW defence of NATO fleets. Just prior to the Falklands action Lt Crudgington had been practising mountain flying at RAF Lossiemouth in Scotland. Culdrose training had included exercises with submarines, low-level navigation, and in-

strument flying, using a dark visor to simulate no-visibility conditions. Recalled from leave, 826 was aboard Hermes within 24 hours, and sailing within 48 hours. From Ascension Island onward the Sea Kings flew a 'ripple' programme of patrols, with two or three aircraft in the air at all times. Each crew flew watches of four hours, with ten hours between watches.

Crewed by two pilots, an observer and a crewman (whose job was to operate the sonar and the rescue winch), three Sea Kings from Hermes flew large numbers of routine patrols once inside Falklands waters, looking out for surface boats and submarines within the Hermes' area. They also flew anti-surface patrols around the west coast of West Island towards the end of May. At one point Paul Crudgington was involved in taking men off the stricken Atlantic Conveyor and Sheffield. On the day of the surrender he ferried VIPs into Stanley for the formal surrender ceremony.

After the Falklands he took a Helicopter Warfare Instructor's course for four and a half months, returning to 810 Squadron at Culdrose to teach warfare techniques to pilots, observers and crewmen. He also taught basic decking operations to helicopter crews throughout most of 1983 and 1984. For this purpose the Royal Fleet Auxiliary 'Engadine' is used. Engadine is a converted car ferry of considerable age, equipped with a hangar and landing spots for helicopters.

In the first part of 1985 Paul Crudgington took a course at RAF Shorebury in Shropshire to become a Qualified Helicopter Instructor (QHI), a qualification which he now employs in 706 Squadron, teaching the Sea King to pilots who have just won their wings on Gazelles.

From Gazelles to Sea Kings

A typical day's training with 706 Squadron would include two or three instructional sorties of up to two hours' duration, over land or sea according to the phase of training. Each sortie is bracketed by a briefing and a debriefing, in addition to which the instructor has to write his report on the student's progress. The students have made the big jump from the training Gazelles of 705 to the dauntingly large and complex Sea Kings of 706, and are doing up to four hours training a day, for five days a week. At this stage of training the students, all of whom already have their wings, will complete some 70 hours flying time in 706, and will then progress to operational training with 810 Squadron, learning the techniques of sea-based flying with the aid of the Engadine.

Each training flight is preceded by an hour's briefing, followed by the study of MOD form 700, the document containing the running technical report on the individual aircraft, with details of fuelling, repairs, and faults. Student and instructor then carry out an external check of the aircraft, looking for such things as loose panels and low tyre pressures. This is followed by an internal

Lieutenant Paul Crudgington in front of a Naval rescue Wessex helicopter. During the Falklands War, he helped to rescue men from the crippled *Atlantic Conveyor*, and has since returned to qualify as an instructor converting newly-qualified pilots to the Sea King.

check, making sure everything is secure, before climbing into the seats. Instructor and student sit side by side. The student starts the aircraft up, doing all checks, a process that takes about ten minutes. They then taxi out to the runway, lift to a hover, and fly at about 1000 feet to Predannack, the satellite airfield five miles south of Culdrose, if this is to be a general training operation. Predannack will be used as the airfield for the training session, keeping the trainees away from the busy Culdrose traffic.

Sea King sturdy in rough conditions

The exercises carried out could include circuits, and autorotations. This is a safety technique for landing in the event of an engine malfunction. The aim is to induce an airflow through the rotors which creates an autorotation sufficient to allow a reasonably controlled landing. Another emergency simulated in these training sessions is the malfunction of one of the two hydraulic systems which help the aircraft to fly. It is still possible to fly the aircraft – albeit with difficulty – on a single hydraulic system.

The Sea King's major advantage over other helicopters is its excellent hovering and low level operations capability, even in bad weather. The technical wizardry which gives the Sea King this capability also makes it a difficult aircraft to handle if anything goes wrong. For this reason a large amount of training is taken up with emergency procedures of one sort and another. At a late stage of the course the students practice hovering low over the sea at night, carrying out one or two sorties of two hours each every twenty-four hours.

In 1984 Paul Crudgington took part in exercises off Portugal, with the Sea Kings based on the Engadine. The training exercises were for the Sea King's primary task of anti-submarine warfare, and involved the use of the aircraft's detection systems. There are two of these, both sonar, the one active, the other passive. Both are operated by the aircrew man. The active system works by sending pulses through the water which bounce off submarine shells and are then picked up again. Having been given the position of a suspected submarine, the pilots, both of whom are needed if anything goes wrong with the helicopter, station the aircraft in the right position and hover, usually at about 40 feet above the surface of the sea, though if the sea is rough they keep it higher so that the engines cannot suck in damaging salt spray. The sonar transducer is lowered up to 200 feet into the water.

With the passive sonar system, the aircraft first of all drops sonar buoys around the area where a submarine is suspected to be. The information coming back from these buoys, which have a limited battery life and are not recovered, is collated in the aircraft with the help of hand-held computers. The ASW Sea Kings also carry depth charges, and so can both seek and destroy submarines when operating in a state of war, though they are limited in their strike power by considerations of weight.

The Sea King can fly without refuelling for up to five hours, though this is reduced if the aircraft does much hovering as this uses up more power and therefore more fuel – half as much again as normal flying.

Over the waves ... and under

Every three or four months Lt Paul Crudgington has to begin from scratch with a new set of students. As well as training these pilots, he also has a completely different role as a diver. Starting in 1978 he trained as a ship's diving officer, and as a search and rescue diver. One function of the helicopter-borne diver is to be in attendance when ship-based aircraft such as Harriers are taking off and landing. The diver sits in the doorway of the helicopter, and in the event of an accident can be in the sea in seconds to help the crew of ditched aircraft. Paul Crudgington dives a minimum of ten times a year, usually around the Cornish coast. In 1984 he dived in both Florida and the Bahamas. In addition to his other duties, he now helps train divers at Culdrose.

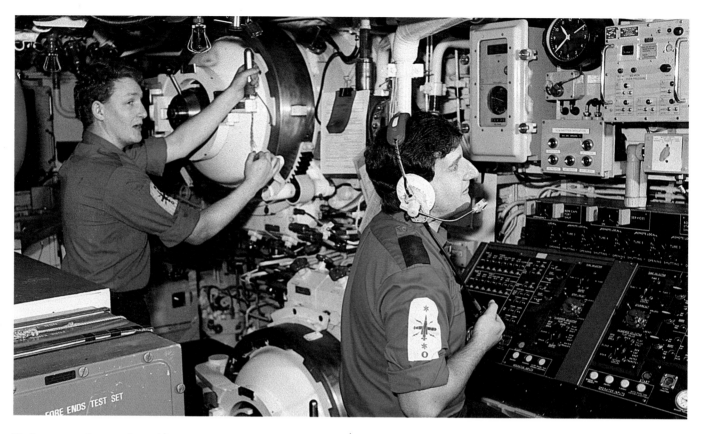

if there can be such a thing as space on a submarine where cramped living is an essential feature of life.

"Only the Captain has a cabin to himself, and even that's no more than six feet square. The other officers double up and the rest of us have a tiny bunk space and a locker for our entire belongings".

Britain's independent strategic nuclear deterrent is currently maintained by the Polaris-equipped ballistic missile submarines, or 'bombers', of the *Resolution* class. Carrying up to 140 officers and men, the nuclear-powered SSBNs are designed to afford a degree of comfort to offset the long patrols lasting three months or more. Medical facilities, separate messes and a well-supplied cinema help to make life aboard more tolerable. Three storeys high, the Polaris submarine is about ten times the size of its World War II counterpart, the U-boat.

For the crews, the sinister implications of their job are an aspect they rarely consider, at least outwardly, since the use of their 16 missiles would automatically mean the destruction of their own homes and lives on shore – either as a retaliatory action or as a first strike. It is just another job to do, and the routine nature of patrols and exercises helps to keep the reality at an acceptable distance.

Unlike the patrol submarines, the 'bombers' operate to a regular schedule with two weeks – one at sea, one in port, so at least they can to some extent plan ahead for holidays and family occasions, although for security reasons exact dates of departure and, more importantly, returns are kept secret from all but a few until the last moment.

Above: Fore-ends of HMS *Trafalgar* with torpedo firing control panel and two tubes visible. *Trafalgar* class Fleet submarines carry either Tigerfish torpedoes or Stonefish and Urchin mines.

Coming Home

"Straw, that's what fresh air smells like – its quite a strong smell, too". After 2 months at sea, submerged and, for all but a few senior crew, wholly unaware of where you are, the effects of re-surfacing can be quite marked for a nuclear submariner.

"I always avoid driving for a few days after we come back, because after weeks of being able to look no further than a few yards, the sudden change to long vision can confuse the eyes. Its difficult to anticipate traffic light changes, for instance, or judge when a person crossing the road ahead of you is going to be clear. Your perspective needs time to adjust".

Other effects of a submariner's life are less physical than mental. Surprisingly, though, claustrophobia is a rare condition despite the fact that there are over a hundred men crammed together in a steel tube underwater for many weeks, without contact from home. "We get a sort of news digest sent out from London – drawn from the Telegraph and carefully edited, and short 'family-gram' messages from home". Really bad news, like death in the family, is kept back by the Captain.

"You can opt to be told after docking, or a day before, which is probably just as well as there's usually nothing you can do beforehand except worry".

With the absolute lack of any daylight, sense of time on board can become distorted, or disappear altogether.

Above: Maintenance work on one of HMS *Trafalgar's* Sub Harpoon practice missiles. Below: HMS *Tireless*, most recent of the *Trafalgar* class boats, on the launching ramp at Vickers Shipbuilders. The new Trafalgar class is intended to replace the *Valiant* class by the end of the decade. The US-developed Sub-Harpoon system is designed for submarine launch against surface targets. Launched from standard tubes it gives the Navy a first-time over-the-horizon missile capability, with extra helicopter-controlled guidance.

"We usually catch a couple of hours kip between watches, whenever the need arises really, or the opportunity, as your sense of day and night soon disappears. Sometimes red lighting is switched on to remind everyone that it is night time – GMT, of course – but it doesn't make much difference". One way to distinguish the division of the day is by meal times – an important antidote to the monotony of a long patrol. "At first its all fresh meat and salads, or on the rare occasions when we put in at a foreign port, but after a while everything is replaced with tinned stuff as stocks begin to run low".

There is an undefined division between those who sail in the big "nukes" and other submarines, a sort of mutual disrespect born out of a sense of "cushiness" these big and relatively modern boats are seen as having, in contrast to the awesome destructive power packed in the tubes along their backs. Despite these accusations of softness, a submariner's life is certainly a unique one in today's navy. For some, it is nothing more than a spell in an "underwater sewer pipe", but for others it is a way of life that offers excitement, challenge and . . . that special quality which makes an elite.

Chapter 7

FORCES DIARY: REVIEW OF THE YEAR

Forces Diary examines some of the major events, both public and military, which have played a significant part in Forces life of the preceding year, and glances ahead to some activities in the coming year.

Live firing at the Royal Artillery Larkhill Open Day. Events like this tend to reinforce positive aspects of the relationship between Forces and public.

Michael Heseltine MP, the present Secretary of State for Defence will probably be the first to admit that managing the nation's Defence programme is rather like learning to play the violin in public. As long as reducing the Public Sector Borrowing Requirement remains a single long-term objective of the Thatcher Government, it is imperative that any public money spent on Defence is well spent. Throughout the British Forces, the control of expenditure has been felt at both the paper clip and the advanced weapon technology end of an enormous spectrum of activity.

1985 was not, in fact, a year for major new initiatives in the Defence arena. In UK terms, the expansion of the Territorial Army, representing a cost-effective method of getting reasonably well trained reinforcement troops to the BAOR combat zone, was re-emphasised and further consolidated. Supporting American policy initiatives in the extraordinarily contentious field of nuclear arms talks at Geneva with the Soviet Union was another important area of consideration that the government was keen to bring to public awareness – as was making affirmatory noises about the American's Strategic Defence Initiative, or 'Star Wars' policy. Stepping up the number of review body and study activities involving in-depth research into manpower and equipment needs also played a visible part. So did looking into the possibilities of tendering a great many military establishment business concerns – predominantly in the support units – to civilian contractors. But whilst the government was keen to project a dynamic and forward-looking policy, aimed at increasing the fighting strength of the Armed Forces, the main concerns were inevitably to do with available cash for the purpose.

In March 1985 the Ministry of Defence announced its initiatives concerning the streamlining and reshaping of the Army in terms of manpower and equipment as well as concerning important strategic refinements of the frontline activities in the Federal Republic of Germany. The name of the initiative was Exercise Lean Look which describes in a nutshell the purpose of the enterprise. An open Government document published in March outlines the primary objective as follows:

> "... increasing the money devoted to defence is only one way of increasing the capabilities of our Armed Forces. Another, and a crucially important task, is to obtain better value from the resources we invest in defence ..."

Just how that important task is intended to be carried out is briefly described below. Also outlined are some of the important activities that took place in 1985 including major exercises, international equipment exhibitions and the major force and equipment enhancements that affect the strength or strategic balance of the British Armed Forces' commitments both at home and overseas.

Exercise LEAN LOOK

By the end of this Financial Year (1985-1986) defence

Above: Prince Andrew with Civil Commissioner Sir Rex Hunt meets women and men of the Falklands Defence Force during the opening ceremony of the new airport at Mount Pleasant in 1985. Expensive to build, it will enable long-term savings.

expenditure, excluding costs relating to the hefty British commitment to the Falklands Garrison (with a revised 1985 estimate of £270 million to be spent on the new airstrip alone), will be nearly a fifth higher than it was when the Conservative government came to power. In 1985-86 terms this means more than an extra billion pounds will be spent by April. With the Army's equipping, manning and training costs, the purpose of Lean Look is to bring effective management of this money to bear in all areas of activity.

– extending contracts placed with civil firms for the maintenance of Army training aircraft at Middle Wallop, as well as for other services at the Army Air Corps Headquarters there;

– reducing the number and size of Army bands.

1985 saw other major rationalisations too. Where, in the past, each of the three main services had its own cookery, driving, musician and language training facilities, these have now been centralised in a single joint services educational establishment: cookery training at Aldershot, service musician training at Deal, driving at Portsmouth, and the Defence Language School at Beaconsfield. In 1986 plans are already being seriously considered for the combining, possibly even the privatising, of the major Veterinary Schools at which, in areas such as dog training, a good deal of activity is already carried out on a joint service footing.

To further these achievements, Exercise Lean Look carries the intention of shifting an extra 4,000 soldiers from support units to frontline activities (which represents about 3% of the total trained manpower) and sending with them all the necessary logistic support. The intention is to bring down the overall numbers of the trained adult male soldier establishment to about 137,000, arriving at this figure sometime in 1987.

Exercise Lean Look is, not surprisingly, the result of an enormous amount of committee work and research activity – there were a total of 22 studies making up the most comprehensive assessment of its kind carried out for years. One thing that all the various studies, which ranged from the assessment of important individual posts to the examination of entire units, clearly indicated was the possibility of employing civilians in places which had been purely the orbit of military personnel – particularly in clerical and administrative roles. As well as cutting (or 'saving' as governmental legalese likes to put it) certain posts, Exercise Lean Look is concerned with enhancing numbers of men in frontline activities and improving and updating the equipment they use. Thus the objective appears to be to maximise the Army's fighting strength within the numbers available.

Contracting Out

Many of the tail units that are to be streamlined will go to civilian contractors, which means that the same money will be spent but it will go from the public to the private sector and bring in tax and job benefits there. The Royal Corps of Transport will soon be dealt with in this way. In 1985 the RCT remained the formation of a large number of soldiers employed to manage, drive and maintain various Army vehicles including staff cars, vans, minibuses, coaches and lorries which, it is judged, could be a service provided just as effectively by civilian contractors. Starting in 1986, quite a few of these services will go to contractors and many more will follow.

In the same manner, the precedent of having four civilian catering contracts for UK static units will be used to extend a further 29 tenders to civilian firms.

In the period from 1981 to 1985, the trained adult male soldier establishment was reduced from 142,000 to 139,000 with no reduction in the overall number of major combat units – and an increased South Atlantic commitment. Principally, the process of whittling down numbers has been brought about by the following means:

– rationalising the Army's training organisation, following intensive reviews;
substituting civilians for military personnel in over 400 military posts;
– restructuring the British Army of the Rhine;
– introducing civilian contract caterers in 4 static units which has proved more cost-effective;
– cutting logistics services by 400 posts;

RICHARD SCOLLINS 1985

The Royal Army Ordnance Corps Central Depots represents a beehive of military supply activity with hundreds of thousands of military articles from teaspoons to replacement aiming units for Milan Anti-tank guided missiles – equipment sent all over the world every day. These depots will be increasingly administered by civilian contractors as will many of the tasks at present undertaken by the Army Quartermasters.

In a similar vein, static communications facilities, which for the Navy and RAF have already largely been contracted out, will be handed over to civilian contractors. And it is likely that 1986 will see the diminishment of the Royal Army Dental Corps' activities at Aldershot although there will still be trained dental officers in uniform at Regimental posts throughout the Army. Dental technicians in the highly professional Prosthetics department will have their work contracted out to civilians.

Finally, before moving out by air to an exercise or operation Army units are concentrated at the Army Mounting Centre, South Cerney, and civilian contracts will be invited to tender for security, catering and mess facilities.

These are the principal means by which Lean Look will be further shaping the Army's already lean body. There are secondary, but equally telling means by which this form of exercise will tone the Army muscle. For example . . .

... More Servicewomen
Lean Look studies examined how women were employed by the Army and found savings in various posts where women could replace men so that the 'tail to teeth' flow can be speeded up. Most of the posts concerned are those in clerical, communications and movement control areas in the support units. Part of these studies went in identifying exactly how women's career structures could be made more attractive by bringing in extra responsibilities and challenges.

... New Technology
Whilst the term 'New Technology' causes a dread amongst unions in the private sector, the Army is looking forward to adopting it wherever there is a chance of saving manpower. The PTARMIGAN secure trunk communications system is, for example, a very expedient alternative to the existing manpower heavy combat net radio system and wherever ADP (Automatic Data Processing) systems can be introduced to facilitate the control of supplies and stocks, they will be.

... The Supernumerary Allowance
It has been policy within the Army to include a number of additional men who are deployed when soldiers be-

Royal Signals radio operator with Ptarmigan communications system. Ptarmigan is an Automatic Data Processing system which will lighten and simplify existing net radio systems.

come 'non-effective'; that is, when they're on long training courses, long-term sick leave, embarkation or terminal leave. This is known as the Supernumerary Allowance and part of Lean Look's remit is to reduce numbers by 20% without effecting operational capability. About 1,000 posts will go this way.

On the other hand: Enhancements

For those who are keen to see a strong, well maintained and active Army continuing into the 90s, Exercise Lean Look is by no means all bad news. Some of the extra billion pounds, representing a real increase in the 1986 Defence budget of about 3%, will be spent on enhancing the Army's capability in terms of new equipment and new forces in strategically important areas. The following areas in particular will benefit.

Armoured warfare

An additional armoured regiment will be formed, the 12th, in BAOR making an increase of four times the number stationed there in 1979. This will enable the new Challenger tank to be more effectively deployed and thermal imaging equipment and additional manpower will complement this force.

Close combat

A new mechanised combat vehicle, the MCV80, will

Right: MCV 80 (Mechanised Combat Vehicle) is not a tank, rather an armoured Infantry vehicle. Below: Trident submarines under construction in the US. Despite the savings on Lean Look, massive Government spending is predicted for the replacement of Polaris.

equip all mechanised battalions and there will be additional manpower deployed to operate them. Mechanised battalions based in the UK, destined to reinforce those in the BAOR, will be equipped with the latest SAXON wheeled personnel carrier.

Fire support

The Royal Artillery has, for years, used the M107 (175mm) large long-distance self-propelled tracked gun and the whole Regiment of guns will be re-equipped with the Multiple Launch Rocket System (MRLS) which has advantages over the M107 both in relation to depth of fire and weight of fire.

Air defence

Nearly a quarter of the new posts created in the Air Defence role will be deployed to increase protection of our ground forces in the event of air attack – a possibility that has caused a great deal of head-scratching in senior strategic circles. The government is still funding the development of a new High Velocity Missile which will be deployed with a new Close Air Defence Regiment in Germany. The intention is to use this missile eventually throughout the combat zone allowing for a more effective use of manpower than has ever been achieved.

Command and control

The new Close Air Defence Regiment will be integrated with the Rapier and Javelin forces and NATO air forces within an Air Defence Command and Information System. Various new technologies are being introduced to allow existing conventional forces to respond to a wider range of operational situations.

Aviation

The present Army Air Corps enemy armour attack establishment is strained into a tight corset, restricted by a deficiency in manpower from acting with full effect. For 1986, new posts are planned that will allow existing forces to greatly increase the number of attack missions by speeding up refuelling and rearming processes for anti-tank helicopters in dispersed hides.

Mobility

Since the formation of the 10th, 11th and now 12th armoured regiment, there is an increased need for armoured engineer support. All operations in the forward combat zone rely on rapid deployment and the armoured engineer support is integral to this concept, hence the Government intends to squeeze more engineers into the frontline activities.

Right: MLRS will provide NATO – and British Forces in particular – with an accurate battlefield missile bombardment system used in conjunction with 'smart' homing warheads and laser target designation.

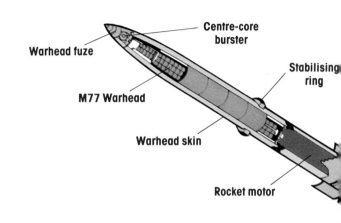

Multiple Launch Rocket S

Warhead fuze

Centre-core burster

Stabilising ring

M77 Warhead

Warhead skin

Rocket motor

Rock
Vent

Azimuth Transmissio
Launcher Drive Syste
and Electronics Unit
(all inside bed)

Aerials for Receiver/Transmitter VRC-46
(in cab)

Thermal battery

Front plate

Driving lights

Access door to
driver/operator
cab

Drive sprocket

m (MLRS)

s (folding)

Boom extension
and actuators

Launch pod/container
hoist (inside assembly)

Launch pod

Launcher Loader Module,
including Fire Control Unit
and Stabilisation Reference
Package

Elevation arm
(hydraulic)

Electronics container
and Boom Controller

Track tension
wheel

Track

mmand box

Return roller

Torsion suspension
bar road wheel arm

Road wheel

Ammunition supply

The frontline will need the quick and ready supply of huge tonnages of ammunition for heavy armoured regiments in the period of transition to war. A new vehicle-based logistic system will help move considerable tonnages in the future. The system is known as the Demountable Rack Offloading and Pick Up System (DROPS) and together with a small increase in manpower it will allow enormous quantities of ammunition to be moved in the combat zone without undue and heavy reliance on Pioneer labour.

Expanding the Territorial Army

The expansion of the TA and other reserve forces has long been a government prerogative – the American system of territorial reserve force training has to some extent set the style and been a successful precedent for this programme. The plan is to increase Britain's TA forces from the existing level of about 76,000 to 86,000 by 1990. This will involve the formation of six new infantry battalions:–

- 1st Battalion The Yorkshire and Cleveland (Volunteers)
- 8th Battalion The Light Infantry (Volunteers)
- 3rd Battalion The Devon and Cornwall Rifle (Volunteers)
- 3rd (Volunteer) Battalion The Cheshire Regiment
- 5th (Volunteer) Battalion The Royal Green Jackets
- 8th (Volunteer) Battalion The Queen's Fusiliers (City of London)

These names were approved by Her Majesty the Queen early in 1985 and their formation is due to start in 1986.

Hosted by the Territorial Army there is to be an increase in the Home Service Force (HSF) to a projected strength of about 5,000 volunteers. This force is set up to provide guard troops for lower-priority potential targets in times of tension or war, enabling higher trained forces to be deployed for other tasks.

The Royal Naval Reserve

This is due for an even greater percentage increase announced by the government at the end of 1984 when the strength was only 5,226. More than 40% extra manpower will eventually bring this figure up to 7,800 – about 12% of the Royal Navy's wartime manpower manning 60% of the Mine Counter Measures (MCM) vessels. Increases are intended in Medical Services within the RNR as well as in the Communications Branch. 1985 in fact was a significant year as far as a recruitment drive across the board was concerned. The same is true of the Royal Marine Reserve requiring more men to provide additional support for 3 Commando Brigade RM and for the Royal Naval Auxiliary Service (RNXS) who are uniformed civilian volunteers mostly recruited in major ports and seaboard areas.

The Royal Auxiliary Airforce

Trained in a wide spectrum of communications and ground support activities, including intelligence work, aerial photo interpretation and message handling, the Royal Auxiliary Air Force is increasingly proving an effective unit within RAF command. In 1985 the government announced the formation of an operational helicopter squadron as soon as resources could be put up. There is already an operative Aeromedical Evacuation Squadron and an Auxiliary Air Movements Squadron within the force and to this a new squadron was added in 1985 to operate the captured Argentinian Skyguard anti-aircraft system, formed at RAF Waddington.

Major Exercises

British Forces continue to take part in exercises around the world, as well as combined NATO force competitions and the training programmes. About every four years a large scale, usually very expensive but extremely instructive exercise is carried out at which NATO and British Forces, including reserves all play a role. Naturally in recent years the emphasis has been on the defence capability of the European front against possible Warsaw Pact confrontation.

Left: 7.62 General Purpose Machinegun on an FV432 armoured personnel carrier of the 3rd Battalion, Royal Anglian Regiment east of Hildesheim during Lionheart. Protection and mobility of troops during the initial stages of a deployment in North Germany are of crucial importance to the reinforcement of the NATO presence in Europe in the event of hostilities.

Exercise LIONHEART

In 1980 Exercise CRUSADER showed up the numerous pitfalls as well as possibilities of getting reinforcements to the frontline zones. This was followed in September 1984 by another massive British Forces initiative, Exercise LIONHEART. The existing BAOR force stands at about 55,000 men which will become 56,000 men by the end of the decade with the intention of providing a structure capable of fielding a total of 150,000 men in time of war, as rapidly and effectively as possible. LIONHEART was set up to test this capability and to point the way to further necessary strategic improvements in forces and equipment to get the daunting process of rapid deployment right.

Apart from demonstrating that rapid reinforcement of this kind was clearly feasible, and therefore maintaining and enhancing Britain's effective commitment to NATO and European Defence, LIONHEART proved the worthiness and serviceability of major equipments. In particular, the Challenger, Saxon, MCV80 and tracked Rapier equipments – all on exercise for the first time – exceeded all expectations.

In order to secure this effective reinforcement, 1985 saw a restructuring of 1(BR) Corps by moving more capability into the forward zones. Two of the three regular armoured divisions have been moved forward. There are now 12 armoured regiments: five equipped with Challenger and the rest with improved Chieftains. These tanks will gradually be fitted out with new thermal imaging sights presently under development. Milan anti-tank missiles will also be issued to all reinforcing infantry battalions and it will itself be fitted with new thermal imaging sights and an improved warhead.

Above: M-2 Abrams Infantry Fighting Vehicle of the US 2nd Army acting as Orange, or Soviet, forces during Lionheart. Below: RAF Jaguar ready at dispersal point during Exercise Coldfire, the air combat equivalent to Lionheart.

Exercise BRAVE DEFENDER

In May 1983, after a decision by the UK Commanders in Chief to undertake a Home Defence Exercise in 1985, planning commenced for what was, effectively, the UK equivalent of LIONHEART. Exercise BRAVE DEFENDER was the first joint service exercise involving the Royal Navy, the Royal Marines, the Army and the Royal Marines, the reserve forces (including the new Home Defence Force). The purpose was to establish the feasibility of effectively guarding Britain against attack. The main potential threat was not judged to be a large-scale invasion but the incursion by small groups of Soviet Troops specially trained in sabotage techniques. Necessarily, United States forces were also deployed to guard one of their Airfield complexes and a Logistics Depot. Target areas for potential saboteurs are barracks, airfields, communication centres including radar bases, and ports.

The exercise took place between the 2nd and 13th September 1985 in three phases:

- 2-6 September, setting up logistic support and enemy role troops and an Umpire Control Organisation in each district.
- 6-8 September, mobilising and deploying Home Defence Forces. The RNR and HSF conducted and completed their defence of the key points mentioned above.
- 9-13 September, follow-up Home Defence activities included defending Key Points and associated ground defence areas; reinforcing these with Mobile Reaction Forces; deploying and using 5 Airborne Brigade.

A total of more than 65,000 troops took part all of whom were drawn from troops committed to the defence of Britain so there was no clash of interest with the number who would, as in LIONHEART, be sent to the German front.

The whole operation involved mobilisation of troops on a totally new scale. The media, in the form of national and regional television were invited to cover various aspects of this mobilisation, particularly with regard to the deployment of reserve forces which involved the consent of thousands of employers. Reservists were followed by press coverage from the office to the drill hall, to the field. A total of 15,000 reserve forces took part. To some extent the police force was also involved mainly by giving practical, traffic flow help at key points and the Department of Transport was also involved at this level. Some of the troops earmarked to reinforce the BAOR were used to play the role of saboteur groups, the BAOR also sent eight companies from the teeth arm to act as enemy troops as well as 110 Umpire Teams. There were a small number of Special Forces involved but their number were few compared with the 16 battalions' worth of enemy forces.

As with Exercise LIONHEART the lessons learnt from this novel kind of exercise will be turned around

and examined in detail for a long time. One thing was certainly proved, the Territorial Army is an invaluable and very credible force to be reckoned with and the media exposure gained has already shown mileage in recruitment enquiries.

The following table shows the breakdown of troops deployed on Exercise BRAVE DEFENDER; the numbers shown include figures for enemy forces, for the umpire organisation and control organisation for the exercise. These numbers represent the planned numbers in mid-1985, not the actual total represented which may differ slightly:

ROYAL NAVY	Regulars	2000	
	RNR & RNXS	2000	Total: 4000
ROYAL MARINES	Regulars	2000	
	RMR	500	Total: 2500
ARMY	Regulars	23000	
	TA	7000	
	HSF	2500	
	Reservists	2500	Total: 35000

Left: A member of the newly formed Home Service Force takes up a defensive position in a well-barricaded house. Field training exercise Brave Defender will provide the first large scale test of such forces. Above: Tornado ADV (F.2) carrying four Skyflash missiles, two sidewinders, and two drop tanks. Tornado aircraft are currently replacing the Jaguars and Buccaneers based in Germany.

Below: RAF logistic support Puma helicopter on exercise in Germany during Coldfire in 1984.

ROYAL AIR	Regular	23000	
FORCE	R Aux AF	500	Total: 23500

RAF Germany

Eight squadrons of Tornado aircraft introduced since 1984 will greatly enhance RAF Germany's strike/attack capability. These will replace the Buccaneers and Jaguars used at present. Already there are six squadrons of Tornado GRI strike/attack craft in service in Germany, the seventh will be introduced this year (1986). The Tornado is equipped with terrain-following radar and advanced avionic and weapon delivery systems and gives RAF Germany a significant improvement in its day-and-night, all-weather low-level capability. The Tornado's effectiveness was more than proved in two major international competitions. Six Tornado aircraft supported by three Victor tankers competed in the annual United States Air Force Strategic Air Command bombing competition against USAF B52s and F111s. Missions involving both simulated and live weapon releases were flown, also the evasion of electronic warfare threats and in flight refuelling – the RAF gained two first places, two seconds and one third in the three trophy events. The competition was run by USAF designed for American aircraft using American techniques so the RAF's success was no mean achievement.

Tornado aircraft fitted with advanced infra-red and video-recording equipment will form later this decade to make a vital part of the reconnaissance squadron and the new Air-Launched Anti-Radiation Missile (ALARM) will be brought in to help create a corridor into Warsaw Pact territory for low-level Tornado missions. To complement the strike/attack force two squadrons of Harrier aircraft will be used in close support of Army ground forces and are able to operate from dispersed hidden sites, which increases their survivability from attacks by Warsaw Pact aircraft. The new GR5 Harrier with complex electronic warfare and countermeasures equipment and a high weapon load capacity will be brought into service.

Finally, together with Rapier-equipped RAF regiment units defending ground forces and installations from air attack, there are to be two squadrons of support helicopters – one Puma and one Chinook – supplying in-theatre logistic and tactical air transport. The Chinooks lost in the Falklands Campaign in 1982 were finally replaced last year, bringing the number up to its full establishment.

New ships for the Royal Navy

The following ships were accepted into service in 1985:

HMS *Tireless* – an anti-submarine warfare (ASW) nuclear-powered Fleet submarine making the total number in service 14 with a further three on order or under construction.

HMS *Ark Royal* – the third Invincible class carrier was accepted in the summer of 85 and will become operational this year. This will mean that two carriers can be operational with the other in refit or reserve all the time.

The following replacement vessels were ordered or tendered:

A new concept AOR (Auxiliary Oiler Replenishment) ship was put out for competitive tender in March 1985. This is a one-stop replenishment vessel carrying fuel, ammunition and stores and also providing aviation sup-

Below: The new through-deck Harrier carrier, HMS *Ark Royal*, third ship of the *Invincible* class during her sea trials. Right: HMS *Tireless*, the latest in the line of nuclear-powered Fleet submarines of which HMS *Trafalgar* is the lead ship.

port for the Type 23 frigate. In the first instance, two of these have been tendered for.

In addition to the actual vessels built or on order there are new equipments to be brought into service including the advanced Type 911 tracker radars first fitted to HMS Brave in October 1984, new small calibre (30mm) canons to replace the long-service Oerlikon and Bofor guns, nine more Sea Harriers put on order for the carrier vessels, new hull-mounted sonar equipment for surface ships and submarines. And the on-going saga of the Nimrod maritime reconnaisance aircraft modernisation is likely to end early this year with the completion of the programme ensuring an instrument which keeps pace with developments in Soviet submarine design.

On a combined, RAF, Royal Navy and merchant shipping basis steps have been taken to ensure that there is an effective air-to-air refuelling and tanker/transport capability so that operations can if necessary be carried out in distant theatres round the globe. MOD policy has been to steadily reduce numbers (see *Forces '85*) around the world whilst maintaining and defending areas of legitimate interest and contributing to the maintenance of international peace on a continued basis. Consideration is being given to a replacement programme for the Victor tanker force (the Victor fared extremely well in the USAF competition) since these aircraft have been in service since the mid 1960s.

Events and exhibitions

The activities of 1985, particularly in terms of the number of presentations and public events, Army, RAF and

Above: A powerful combination. Royal Navy Sea Harrier armed with Sea Eagle anti-shipping missile. Once launched, Sea Eagle drops to just above wave-height to reduce chance of detection.

Royal Navy open days and exhibitions, reveal the high state of morale, and a sense of optimism and purpose which has grown with the present government's commitment to strengthening the Armed Forces and giving them a high public profile. The recent move to involve journalists directly with the major defence activities such as LIONHEART and BRAVE DEFENDER has leant a certain amount of openness to MOD proceedings which have previously been hidden from public knowledge, or wrested into light with difficulty. The events and exhibitions briefly outlined here served both to bring the credibility and effort of the British Forces directly to the public eye, and to forge closer links between individual units and the communities they serve and from which they so often draw their recruits.

NAVY DAYS

June	
8	Scottish International Air Show (HMS GANNET) RN Aircraft Yard Fleetlands Open Day, Hampshire
8-9	Rosyth Navy Days
14	South Atlantic Campaign Memorial Unveiling Ceremony, St Paul's Cathedral, London
July	
10-27	Royal Tournament, Earls Court, London
20	HMS DAEDALUS Air Day, Gosport, Hampshire
20-21	Portland Open Days, Portland Naval Base, Dorset
31	RNAS CULDROSE International Air Day, Helston, Cornwall
August	
3	RNAS YEOVILTON International Air Day, Ilchester, Somerset
9-13	Edinburgh Tattoo
24/25/26	Portsmouth Navy Days Plymouth Navy Days
September	
5-14	RN Equipment Exhibition, HMS EXCELLENT, Whale Island, Nr Portsmouth
October	
16	Annual Seafarer's Service, St Paul's Cathedral, London

ARMY EVENTS

May	
	FA Cup Final, Wembley
25-27	'Motor 100', Silverstone
June	
1	Welsh 1000, (Wales)
1-2	Chester Tattoo, (NWdist)
4-6	H Div Beating Retreat, (Londist)
5	Queens's Birthday Parade, Belgium
1-13	Quen's Div Beating Retreat, (Londist)
14 June – 6 August	Bisley, (UKLF)
15	Queen's Birthday Parade, (rehearsals 1 & 8 June), (Londist)
17-23	Wembley Pageant, (Londist)
28	QDG Tercentenary Parade, (Edist)
July	
5	Royal Visit, Chester, (NWdist)
5	5 Innis DG Tercntenary, (SWdist)
10-27	Royal Tournament, (Londist)
26-27	Dover Tattoo, (SEdist)
August	
1-10	Cardiff Tattoo, (Wales)
2	Beating Retreat, (NWdist)
3-4	Southport Tattoo, (NWdist)
9-31	Edinburgh Tattoo, (Scotland)
September	
28-29	Cambrian Marches, (Wales)
October	
2-6	Cambrian Marches, (Wales)
November	
9	Lord Mayors Show, (Londist)
9	Festival of Remembrance, (Londist & Scotland)
10	Rembrance Day, (SEdist)
10	Cenotaph Remembrance, (Londist)
23-24	March & Shoot Competition, (NEdist/2 Inf Div)
30	SSAFA Centenary Band Concert, (Scotland)

Right: Red Arrows display team carry out pre-season work-up training at RAF Akrotiri each year in addition to the regular Armament Practice camps.

RAF RED ARROWS, DISPLAYS AND OPEN DAYS

April
21 Estoril
28 Old Warden
May
5 Leeds
6 Jersey
7 Guernsey
11 Biggin Hill
12 Biggin Hill
19 Bridlington
19 Manchester (Barton)
25 Dunkerque Fly-Past
25 Eastbourne
25 Mildenhall
26 Mildenhall

June
1 Morecambe
1 Douglas (Isle of Man)
2 Swanton Morley
2 Henlow
4 Ramsey (Isle of Man)
4 Brighton
5 Shape
6 Shape
6 Peel (Isle of Man)
8 Prestwick
8 Edinburgh
9 Church Fenton
15 Swinderby
15 Coningsby
16 Lotus Cars (Norwich)
21 Brize Norton

21 Scampton
22 Newtownards
22 Halton
29 Chester
29 Woodford
30 North Weald
30 Marham

July
4 Harrogate
6 Duxford
6 Hereford
7 Royal Tournament Fly-Past
7 Humberside
13 Plymouth
13 Fairford
14 Fairford
14 Cranwell
20 Shawbury
21 Silverstone
21 Alconbury
24 Chivenor
25 Weston-Super-Mare
25 Brawdy

August
3 Yeovilton
3 Bournemouth
4 Sanicole
7 Ilfracombe Fly-Past
9 Scarborough
10 Worthing
10 Bentwaters

16 Bristol
17 Hoylake
17 Aldergrove
17 Valley
18 Jurby (Isle of Man)
18 Nottingham
19 Whitby
20 Skegness
21 Broadstairs
21 Cromer
21 Weymouth
23 Sidmouth
24 Southport
24 Teeside
25 Leicester
26 Oulton Broad
26 Eye (Suffolk)
26 West Malling
27 Walsall
29 Monmouth
30 Dartmouth
31 Bex

September
1 Bex
7 Leuchars
7 Finningley
12 Guernsey
12 Jersey
14 Abingdon
14 Lyneham
14 St. Athan
15 Duxford

INDEX

DUNCAN BREWER is a freelance journalist with a background in industrial relations, the new technologies and politics. He served with the RAF in Cyprus during the EOKA emergency and developed a special interest in the Falklands conflict.

CHRISTOPHER CHANT was educated at Oxford and worked on the partwork series *History of the Second World War* and *History of the First World War* before editing the *World War II* series. Now a full-time writer and broadcaster, he specialises in aviation history

CHRISTOPHER DOBSON is a war correspondant and author, winner of the IPC Award of International Journalist of the Year for his coverage of the Six Day War in the Middle East and the Tet offensive in Vietnam. He currently lectures at the Police Staff College at Bramshill, and is the author of a number of books on terrorism – but prefers fishing.

GILES EMERSON was educated at Oxford, and specialises in Science and Defence-related subjects on a full-time freelance basis. He worked for several years with the Central Office of Information visiting a number of MOD establishments at home and overseas producing publicity and recruitment material.

MARTIN STREETLY is an aviation and electronic warfare historian who has contributed widely to various military and aviation publications, both as writer and technical illustrator.

Picture Credits
Aviation Photos International 17, 135, 137B
G.L. Bound 128/9
British Aerospace 2, 3, 4, 5, 22T, 22B, 24, 2
   82, 83,
84, 88, 90, 91, 92, 93B, 95, 96, 97, 104, 137,
   139B
Cassidy & Leigh 71, 73T, 76, 77T, 81
Courtesy Jack Garnham 18
Courtesy RHQ Parachute Regiment 19
Courtesy RHQ Parachute Regiment 20
CO1 36, 44
LTV Corps 46–47
Crown/Army 136/7
RNAS/Lt. Paul Crudgington 123
DOD 54, 56T, 56C, 58, 59
Mark Dartford 126/7
Barry Ellson 6/7, 87, 89T, 93T, 100, 102, 10
   107B
Sqdn. Ldr. T.A. Harper 101
Peter Holdgate 34, 35
R Humble 41, 42B
IWM 68, 70, 73B
S/Sgt Kelly RAPC 75
Lockheed 48
Mars 8, 9, 10, 12T, 13–15, 38/39, 42T, 43,
   57, 62/63, 67T&B, 72, 77B, 94
Martin Marietta 49, 52
MOD 26/7, 28/9, 30–33, 109, 110, 112/3, 11
   117
Royal Marines 37T, 45
Royal Navy 124
Andrew Seal 37B
Soldier 65, 131
Swan Hunter 138
United States Airforce 50, 56B
United States Army 51, 60
United States Navy 114T, 115
Vought Corporation 133 inset
Westland Helicopters 89B, 107, 108